Fodor's New

Pocket
Savannah &
Charleston

Reprinted from *Fodor's The South*

Fodor's Travel Publications, Inc.
New York • Toronto • London • Sydney • Auckland
www.fodors.com/

Fodor's Pocket Savannah & Charleston

EDITORS: Linda Cabasin, Audra Epstein, David Low

Area Editors: Jane Garvey, Mary Sue Lawrence

Editorial Contributors: Robert Andrews, David Brown, Anastasia Mills, Heidi Sarna, Helayne Schiff, M. T. Schwartzman (Gold Guide editor), Dinah A. Spritzer

Editorial Production: Janet Foley, Linda K. Schmidt

Maps: David Lindroth, *cartographer*; Robert Blake, *map editor*

Design: Fabrizio La Rocca, *creative director*; Lyndell Brookhouse-Gil, *cover design*; Jolie Novak, *photo editor*

Production/Manufacturing: Mike Costa

Cover Photograph: Bob Krist

Copyright

Special Sales

CONTENTS

**5   Midnight in the Garden of Good   107
      and Evil—An Excerpt**

Index   111

Maps

ON THE ROAD WITH FODOR'S

WE'RE ALWAYS thrilled to get letters from readers, especially one like this:

It took us an hour to decide what book to buy and we now know we picked the best one. Your book was wonderful, easy to follow, very accurate, and good on pointing out eating places, informal as well as formal. When we saw other people using your book, we would look at each other and smile.

Our editors and writers are deeply committed to making every Fodor's guide "the best one"—not only accurate but always charming, brimming with sound recommendations and solid ideas, right on the mark in describing restaurants and hotels, and full of fascinating facts that make you view what you've traveled to see in a rich new light.

About Our Writers

Our success in achieving our goals—and in helping to make your trip the best of all possible vacations—is a credit to the hard work of our extraordinary writers.

Since 1992, Savannah and Golden Isles updater **Jane Garvey** has been chasing the ideal food-and-wine match for readers of the *Atlanta Journal-Constitution,* for whom she writes a column on the subject. She also writes for a number of local magazines. She has coauthored a residents' guide to Atlanta, a city in which she has nibbled and sipped for more than 25 years. A former magazine editor and college professor, she now enjoys travel, reading, and writing about Georgia history, hiking, white-water rafting, and a host of other salubrious pursuits.

Mary Sue Lawrence, who added fresh insights to the Charleston chapter, is a freelance writer and editor whose features on travel, entertainment, health, and business have appeared in national and British magazines. A Charlestonian, she lives on the nearby Isle of Palms. She has also contributed to *Fodor's The South's Best Bed & Breakfasts.*

New This Year

We're proud to announce that the American Society of Travel Agents has endorsed Fodor's as its guidebook of choice. ASTA is the world's largest and most influential travel trade association, operating in more than 170 countries, with 27,000 members pledged to adhere to a strict code of ethics reflecting the Society's motto, "Integrity in Travel." ASTA shares Fodor's devotion to providing smart, honest travel information and advice to travlers, and we've long recommended that our readers consult ASTA member agents for the experience and professionalism they bring to the table.

On the Web, check out Fodor's site (www.fodors.com/) for information on major destinations around the world and travel-savvy interactive features. The Web site also lists the 85-plus radio stations nationwide that carry *Fodor's Travel Show,* a live call-in program that airs every weekend. Tune in to hear guests discuss their wonderful adventures—or call in to get answers for your most pressing travel questions.

How to Use This Book

Organization

Up front is **Essential Information,** an easy-to-use section divided alphabetically by topic. Under each listing you'll find tips and information that will help you accomplish what you need to in Savannah and Charleston. You'll also find addresses and telephone numbers of organizations and companies that offer destination-related services and detailed information and publications.

The first chapter in the guide, **Destination: Savannah and Charleston,** helps get you in the mood for your trip. New and Noteworthy cues you in on trends and happenings, What's Where gets you oriented, Great Itineraries presents some special-interest trip ideas, Fodor's Choice showcases our top picks, and Festivals and Seasonal Events alerts you to special events you'll want to seek out.

At the end of the book you'll find a wonderful portrait of Savannah excerpted from the incredibly popular *Midnight in the Garden of Good and Evil,* by John Berendt.

Icons and Symbols

★   Our special recommendations

✕   Restaurant

🏨   Lodging establishment

✕🏨   Lodging establishment whose restaurant warrants a special trip

⚠   Campground

🐥   Good for kids (rubber duckie)

☞   Sends you to another section of the guide for more information

✉   Address

☎   Telephone number

🕐   Opening and closing times

💲   Admission prices (those we give apply to adults; substantially reduced fees are almost always available for children, students, and senior citizens)

Hotel Facilities

We always list the facilities that are available—but we don't specify whether they cost extra: When pricing accommodations, always ask what's included. In addition, assume that all rooms have private baths unless otherwise noted.

Restaurant Reservations and Dress Codes

Reservations are always a good idea; we note only when they're essential or when they are not accepted. Book as far ahead as you can, and reconfirm when you get to town. Unless otherwise noted, the restaurants listed are open daily for lunch and dinner. We mention dress only when men are required to wear a jacket or a jacket and tie.

Credit Cards

The following abbreviations are used: **AE,** American Express; **D,** Discover; **DC,** Diners Club; **MC,** MasterCard; and **V,** Visa.

Don't Forget to Write

You can use this book in the confidence that all prices and opening times are based on information supplied to us at press time; Fodor's cannot accept responsibility for any errors. Time inevitably brings changes, so always confirm information when it matters—especially if you're making a detour to visit a specific place. In addition, when making reservations be sure to mention if you have a disability or are traveling with children, if you prefer a private bath or a certain type of bed, or if you have specific dietary needs or other concerns.

Were the restaurants we recommended as described? Did our hotel picks exceed your expectations? Did you find a museum we recommended a waste of time? If you have complaints, we'll look into them and revise our entries when the facts warrant it. If you've discovered a special place that we haven't included, we'll pass the information along to our correspondents and have them check it out. So send us your feedback, positive *and* negative: e-mail us at editors@fodors.com (specifying the name of the book on the subject line) or write the Savannah and Charleston editor at Fodor's, 201 East 50th Street, New York, New York 10022. Have a wonderful trip!

Karen Cure

Karen Cure
Editorial Director

The Southeastern United States

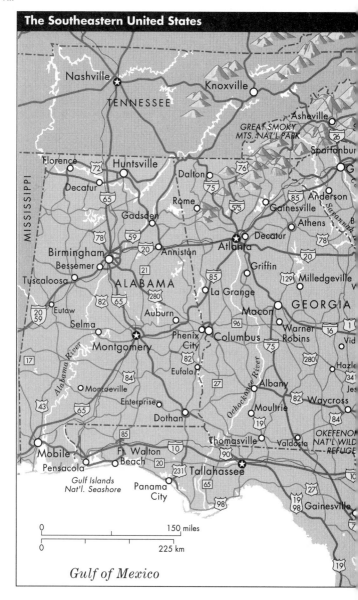

Nashville

Knoxville

TENNESSEE

Asheville

GREAT SMOKY
MTS. NAT'L PARK

Spartanbur

26

Florence

72

Huntsville

Dalton

76

G

MISSISSIPPI

Decatur

65

75

Rome

575

85 Anderson

Gainesville

Savannah

B

Gadsden

Athens

78

78

59

Decatur

Birmingham

20

Anniston

Atlanta

20

Bessemer

21

Griffin

Tuscaloosa

ALABAMA

85

129 Milledgeville

V

82 65

280

La Grange

GEORGIA

20
59

Eutaw

Auburn

Macon

96

Warner
Robins

16

1

Selma

Phenix
City

Columbus

75

Vid

17

Alabama River

Montgomery

82

280

Hazle

84

Eufala

27

Albany

341

Jes

Monroeville

82

Waycross

43

65

Enterprise

Moultrie

84

Dothan

19

OKEFENO
NAT'L WILD
REFUGE

85

Thomasville

Valdosta

Mobile

Ft. Walton

10

90

10

Pensacola

Beach

20

231

Tallahassee

Gulf Islands
Nat'l. Seashore

Panama
City

65

27

98

19
98

Gainesville

Ochoch(ree River

0   150 miles

0   225 km

7

19

Gulf of Mexico

ESSENTIAL INFORMATION

*Basic Information on Traveling in Savannah
and Charleston, Savvy Tips to Make Your Trip
a Breeze, and Companies and Organizations
to Contact*

AIR TRAVEL

Most people choose a flight based on price. Yet there are other issues to consider. Major airlines offer the greatest number of departures; smaller airlines—including regional, low-cost, and no-frill airlines—usually have a more limited number of flights daily. Major airlines have frequent-flyer partners, which allow you to credit mileage earned on one airline to your account with another. Low-cost airlines offer a definite price advantage and fewer restrictions, such as advance-purchase requirements. Safety-wise, low-cost carriers as a group have a good history, but **check the safety record before booking** any low-cost carrier; call the Federal Aviation Administration's Consumer Hotline (☞ Airline Complaints, *below*).

➤ MAJOR AIRLINES: **Air Canada** (☎ 800/776–3000). **American** (☎ 800/433–7300). **America West** (☎ 800/235–9292). **Continental** (☎ 800/525–0280). **Delta** (☎ 800/221–1212). **Northwest Airlines** (☎ 800/225–2525). **TWA** (☎ 800/221–2000). **United**

(☎ 800/241–6522). **US Airways** (☎ 800/428–4322).

➤ SMALLER AIRLINES: **Air South** (☎ 800/247–7688). **American Eagle** (☎ 800/433–7300). **Atlantic Southeast** (☎ 800/221–1212). **Kiwi** (☎ 800/538–5494). **Markair** (☎ 800/521–9854). **Midway** (☎ 888/226–4392). **Midwest Express** (☎ 800/452–2022). **Northwest Airlink** (☎ 800/225–2525). **ValuJet** (☎ 800/825–8538). **Western Pacific** (☎ 800/930–3030).

➤ FROM THE U.K.: **American** (☎ 0345/789789). **British Airways** (☎ 0345/222111). **Delta** (☎ 0800/414767). **United Airlines** (☎ 0800/888–555).

For further information on airports and airlines serving Savannah and Charleston, see their individual chapters.

GET THE LOWEST FARE
The least-expensive airfares to the South are priced for round-trip travel. Major airlines usually require that you **book in advance and buy the ticket within 24 hours,** and you may have to **stay**

over a Saturday night. It's smart to **call a number of airlines, and when you are quoted a good price, book it on the spot**—the same fare may not be available on the same flight the next day. Airlines generally allow you to change your return date for a fee of $25–$50. If you don't use your ticket you can apply the cost toward the purchase of a new ticket, again for a small charge. However, most low-fare tickets are nonrefundable. To get the lowest airfare, **check different routings.** If your destination or home city has more than one gateway, compare prices to and from different airports. Also price off-peak flights, which may be significantly less expensive.

To save money on flights from the United Kingdom and back, **look into an APEX or Super-PEX ticket.** APEX tickets must be booked in advance and have certain restrictions. Super-PEX tickets can be purchased at the airport on the day of departure—subject to availability.

DON'T STOP UNLESS YOU MUST

When you book, **look for nonstop flights** and **remember that "direct" flights stop at least once.** Try to **avoid connecting flights,** which require a change of plane. Two airlines may jointly operate a connecting flight, so ask if your airline operates every segment—you may find that your preferred carrier flies you only part of the way.

USE AN AGENT

Travel agents, especially those who specialize in finding the lowest fares, can be especially helpful when booking a plane ticket. When you're quoted a price, **ask your agent if the price is likely to get any lower.** Good agents know the seasonal fluctuations of airfares and can usually anticipate a sale or fare war. However, waiting can be risky: The fare could go *up* as seats become scarce, and you may wait so long that your preferred flight sells out. A wait-and-see strategy works best if your plans are flexible, but if you must arrive and depart on certain dates, don't delay.

Airlines routinely overbook planes, knowing that not everyone with a ticket will show up, but sometimes everyone does. When that happens, airlines ask for volunteers to give up their seats. In return these volunteers usually get a certificate for a free flight and are rebooked on the next flight out. If there are not enough volunteers the airline must choose who will be denied boarding. The first to get bumped are passengers who checked in late and those flying on discounted tickets, **so get to the gate and check in as early as possible,** especially during peak periods.

Always **bring a photo ID to the airport.** You may be asked to show it before you are allowed to check in.

ENJOY THE FLIGHT

For better service, **fly smaller or regional carriers,** which often have higher passenger-satisfaction ratings. Sometimes you'll find leather seats, more legroom, and better food.

For more legroom, **request an emergency-aisle seat**; don't, however, sit in the row in front of the emergency aisle or in front of a bulkhead, where seats may not recline.

If you have specific dietary needs, **ask for special meals when booking.** These can be vegetarian, low-cholesterol, or kosher, for example.

COMPLAIN IF NECESSARY

If your baggage goes astray or your flight goes awry, complain right away. Most carriers require that you file a claim immediately.

➤ AIRLINE COMPLAINTS: U.S. Department of Transportation **Aviation Consumer Protection Division** (✉ C-75, Room 4107, Washington, DC 20590, ☎ 202/366–2220). Federal Aviation Administration (FAA) Consumer Hotline (☎ 800/322–7873).

AIRPORTS

➤ IN GEORGIA: Numerous international and domestic airlines serve **Hartsfield Atlanta International Airport** (✉ I–85 and I–285, ☎ 404/530–6600), 13 mi south of downtown Atlanta.

The **Macon Municipal Airport** (✉ 4000 Terminal Dr., GA 247 and I–75, ☎ 912/788–3760) is served by Atlantic Southeast Airlines. Eighteen miles west of downtown, **Savannah International Airport** (☎ 912/964–0514) is served by Delta, US Airways, and ValuJet for domestic flights. To reach the Golden Isles by air, **Glynco Jetport** (☎ 800/282–3424), 6 mi north of Brunswick, is served by Delta affiliate Atlantic Southeast Airlines, with flights from Atlanta.

➤ IN SOUTH CAROLINA: Major airports are **Charleston International Airport** (☎ 803/767–1100); **Myrtle Beach International Airport** (☎ 803/448–1589); **Hilton Head Island Airport** (served by US Airways Express); the closest metropolitan airport is **Savannah International Airport** (☎ 912/964–0514), about an hour's drive from Hilton Head; **Columbia Metro Airport** (☎ 803/822–5000); **Greenville-Spartanburg Airport** (☎ 864/867–7426).

BED-AND-BREAKFAST RESERVATIONS

➤ IN GEORGIA: **Georgia Bed & Breakfast** (☎ 770/493–1930) is an agency that can connect you with area lodging (homes, resorts, and inns). **Great Inns of Georgia** (☎ 404/252–8886 or 800-664–7328) can connect you to numerous bed-and-breakfast inns around the state. In addition the bimonthly *Georgia Journal* (✉ Box 1604, Decatur 30031-1604, ☎ 404/377–4275 or 800/268–6942) has extensive lists of restaurants and bed-and-breakfast inns throughout the state.

➤ IN SOUTH CAROLINA: For a complete list of B&Bs, write to the **South Carolina Division of Tourism** (✉ 1205 Pendleton St., Columbia 29201, ☎ 803/734–0122 or 800/872–3505) and ask for the pamphlet *Bed & Breakfast of South Carolina*. Write to the **South Carolina Bed and Breakfast Association** (✉ Box 1275, Sumter 29150-1275) for a current state directory of member B&Bs.

BIKING

With a membership of about 4,000, the **Southern Bicycle League** (✉ Box 1360, Roswell 30077, ☎ 770/594–8350) for more than 20 years has promoted bicycling across Georgia and the South. The **Bicycle Ride Across Georgia (BRAG)** (☎ 770/921–6166) is an annual event.

BUS TRAVEL

➤ BUS LINES: Greyhound (☎ 800/231–2222) operates passenger buses connecting towns and cities in Georgia and South Carolina.

CAMERAS, CAMCORDERS, & COMPUTERS

Always **keep your film, tape, or computer disks out of the sun.** Carry an extra supply of batteries, and **be prepared to turn on your camera, camcorder, or laptop** to prove to security personnel that the device is real. Always **ask for hand inspection of film,** which becomes clouded after successive exposure to airport x-ray machines, and **keep videotapes and computer disks away from metal detectors.**

➤ PHOTO HELP: **Kodak Information Center** (☎ 800/242–2424). *Kodak Guide to Shooting Great Travel Pictures,* available in bookstores or from Fodor's Travel Publications (☎ 800/533–6478); $16.50 plus $4 shipping.

CAR RENTAL

Rates in Atlanta, Georgia, begin at $40 a day and $150 a week for an economy car with air-conditioning, an automatic transmission, and unlimited mileage. This does not include tax on car rentals, which is 5%. These rates are typical of those found in larger cities in the South.

➤ MAJOR AGENCIES: **Alamo** (☎ 800/327–9633; 0800/272–2000 in the U.K.). **Avis** (☎ 800/331–1212; 800/879–2847 in Canada). **Budget** (☎ 800/527–0700; 0800/181181 in the U.K.). **Dollar** (☎ 800/800–4000; 0990/565656 in the U.K., where it is known as Eurodollar). **Hertz** (☎ 800/654–3131; 800/263–0600 in Canada; 0345/555888 in the U.K.). **National InterRent** (☎ 800/227–7368; 0345/222525 in the U.K., where it is known as Europcar InterRent).

➤ RENTAL WHOLESALERS: Contact Auto Europe (☎ 207/828–2525 or 800/223–5555).

CUT COSTS

To get the best deal, **book through a travel agent who is willing to shop around.** When pricing cars, **ask about the location of the rental lot.** Some off-airport locations offer lower rates, and their lots are only minutes from the terminal via complimentary shuttle. You also may want to **price local car-rental companies,** whose rates may be lower still, although their service and maintenance may not be as good as those of a name-brand agency. Remember to ask about required deposits, cancellation penalties, and drop-off charges if you're planning to pick up the car in one city and leave it in another.

Also **ask your travel agent about a company's customer-service record.** How has it responded to late plane arrivals and vehicle mishaps? Are there often lines at the rental counter, and, if you're traveling during a holiday period, does a confirmed reservation guarantee you a car?

NEED INSURANCE?

When driving a rented car you are generally responsible for any damage to or loss of the vehicle. You also are liable for any property damage or personal injury that you may cause while driving. Before you rent, **see what coverage you already have** under the terms of your personal auto-insurance policy and credit cards.

For about $14 a day, rental companies sell protection, known as a collision- or loss-damage waiver (CDW or LDW) that eliminates your liability for damage to the car; it's always optional and should never be automatically added to your bill.

In most states you don't need CDW if you have personal auto insurance or other liability insurance. However, **make sure you have enough coverage to pay for the car.** If you do not have auto insurance or an umbrella policy that covers damage to third parties, purchasing CDW or LDW is highly recommended.

BEWARE SURCHARGES

Before you pick up a car in one city and leave it in another, **ask about drop-off charges or one-way service fees,** which can be substantial. Note, too, that some rental agencies charge extra if you return the car before the time specified on your contract. To avoid a hefty refueling fee, **fill the tank just before you turn in the car,** but be aware that gas stations near the rental outlet may overcharge.

MEET THE REQUIREMENTS

In the United States you must be 21 to rent a car, and rates may be higher if you're under 25. You'll pay extra for child seats (about $3 per day), which are compulsory for children under five, and for additional drivers (about $2 per day). Residents of the United Kingdom will need a reservation voucher, a passport, a U.K. driver's license, and a travel policy that covers each driver, in order to pick up a car.

CAR TRAVEL

➤ IN GEORGIA: Georgia is traversed east and west by several interstate highways. North and south are covered by I–75, running from northwest through the center of the state to the Florida line; I–85 runs from the northeastern part of the state through the west to Alabama; I–95 runs along the Georgia coast from South Carolina to Florida. I–85 and I–75 converge in Atlanta near its downtown; this nexus is called the Connector. Running east and west, I–20 stretches from Birmingham, Alabama, to Augusta, Georgia, running through the center of downtown Atlanta on its way. From Macon, I–16 leads directly east to Savannah, where it ends; along its route lie several interesting towns, including Vidalia (home of the famous onion). Scenic routes include GA 76, a good highway running east–west through the north Georgia mountains, and U.S. 441, running north–south from the mountains to the Florida line. Along the way, U.S. 441 links numerous charming small towns and is lined with barbecue joints of worth. On the western side of the state, various pleasant small towns are connected by U.S. 19, the north–south route of choice prior to development of the interstate and still a good option if I–75 comes to a standstill, as it routinely does Thanksgiving Eve. I–75 also runs through a number of quaint small towns.

The speed limit on interstates is 50 mph in metropolitan areas and 70 mph elsewhere. Right turns on red lights are permitted unless otherwise indicated.

Call the **Georgia Department of Industry, Trade, and Tourism** (⌧ Box 1776, Atlanta 30301, ☎ 404/656–3545 or 800/847–4842, ℻ 404/651–9063) for copies of its brochures and maps. Especially useful is its "Georgia On My Mind," published annually, which includes a map and much valuable information.

For road information, call the **Georgia Department of Transportation** (☎ 404/656–1267).

➤ IN SOUTH CAROLINA: I–26 traverses the state from northwest to southeast and terminates at Charleston. I–77 leads into Columbia from the north. I–26, I–20, and U.S. 1 intersect at Columbia. I–85 provides access to Greenville, Spartanburg, Pendleton, and Anderson. U.S. 17, a north–south coastal route, runs along the coastal edge of the entire state.

The speed limit on interstates is 65 mph. You can turn right during a red light unless otherwise noted by street signs.

CONSUMER PROTECTION

Whenever possible, **pay with a major credit card** so you can cancel payment if there's a problem, provided that you can provide documentation. This is a good practice whether you're buying travel arrangements before your trip or shopping at your destination.

If you're doing business with a particular company for the first time, **contact your local Better Business Bureau and the attorney general's offices** in your state and the company's home state, as well. Have any complaints been filed?

Finally, if you're buying a package or tour, always **consider travel insurance** that includes default coverage (☞ Insurance, *below*).

➤ LOCAL BBBs: Council of Better Business Bureaus (✉ 4200 Wilson Blvd., Suite 800, Arlington, VA 22203, ☎ 703/276–0100, FAX 703/525–8277).

EMERGENCIES

For **police, ambulance and fire emergencies** in either Georgia or South Carolina dial 911.

FISHING

The **Georgia Department of Natural Resources, Game and Fish Division** (✉ 2070 U.S. Hwy. 278, Social Circle 30279, ☎ 770/918–6400) has free pamphlets covering Georgia's regulations and maps suggesting good fishing spots.

INSURANCE

Travel insurance is the best way to **protect yourself against financial loss.** The most useful policies are trip-cancellation-and-interruption, default, medical, and comprehensive insurance.

Without insurance you will lose all or most of your money if you cancel your trip, regardless of the reason. It's essential that you **buy trip-cancellation-and-interruption insurance,** particularly if your airline ticket, cruise, or package tour is nonrefundable and cannot be changed. When considering how much coverage you need, look for a policy that will cover the cost of your trip plus the nondiscounted price of a one-way airline ticket, should you need to return home early. Also **consider default or bankruptcy insurance,** which protects you against a supplier's failure to deliver.

Citizens of the United Kingdom can buy an annual travel-insurance policy valid for most vacations during the year in which it's purchased. If you are pregnant or have a preexisting medical condition, make sure you're covered. According to the Association of British Insurers, a trade association representing 450 insurance companies, it's wise to buy extra medical coverage when you visit the United States.

If you have purchased an expensive vacation, comprehensive insurance is a must. **Look for comprehensive policies that include trip-delay insurance,** which will protect you in the event that weather problems cause you to miss your flight, tour, or cruise. A few insurers sell waivers for preexisting medical conditions. Companies that offer both features include Access America, Carefree Travel, Travel Insured International, and Travel Guard (☞ *below*).

Always **buy travel insurance directly from the insurance company**; if you buy it from a travel agency or tour operator that goes out of business you probably will not be covered for the agency or operator's default—a major risk. Before you make any purchase, **review your existing health and home-owner's policies** to find out whether they cover expenses incurred while traveling.

➤ TRAVEL INSURERS: In the United States, **Access America** (✉ 6600 W. Broad St., Richmond, VA 23230, ☎ 804/285–3300 or 800/ 284–8300), **Carefree Travel Insurance** (✉ Box 9366, 100 Garden City Plaza, Garden City, NY 11530, ☎ 516/294–0220 or 800/ 323–3149), **Near Travel Services** (✉ Box 1339, Calumet City, IL 60409, ☎ 708/868–6700 or 800/

654–6700), **Travel Guard International** (✉ 1145 Clark St., Stevens Point, WI 54481, ☎ 715/345– 0505 or 800/826–1300), **Travel Insured International** (✉ Box 280568, East Hartford, CT 06128-0568, ☎ 860/528–7663 or 800/243–3174), **Travelex Insurance Services** (✉ 11717 Burt St., Suite 202, Omaha, NE 68154- 1500, ☎ 402/445–8637 or 800/ 228–9792, ℻ 800/867–9531), **Wallach & Company** (✉ 107 W. Federal St., Box 480, Middleburg, VA 20118, ☎ 540/687–3166 or 800/237–6615). In Canada, **Mutual of Omaha** (✉ Travel Division, 500 University Ave., Toronto, Ontario M5G 1V8, ☎ 416/598– 4083; 800/268–8825 in Canada). In the United Kingdom, **Association of British Insurers** (✉ 51 Gresham St., London EC2V 7HQ, ☎ 0171/600–3333).

MONEY

ATMS

Before leaving home, make sure that your credit cards have been programmed for ATM use.

➤ ATM LOCATIONS: **Cirrus** (☎ 800/424–7787). **Plus** (☎ 800/ 843–7587).

NATIONAL AND STATE PARKS

➤ IN GEORGIA: Housed under the Georgia Department of Natural Resources, the **Parks, Recreation & Historic Sites** division (✉ 205 Butler St. SE, 30334, ☎ 404/

656–3530 or 800/864–7275 reservations; 770/389–7275 local reservations) has information on Georgia's parks.

➤ IN SOUTH CAROLINA: For information about South Carolina's national parks areas, contact the **U.S. Forest Service** (✉ 4931 Broad River Rd., Columbia 29210, ☎ 803/561–4000). Several of South Carolina's 48 state parks operate like resort communities, with everything from deluxe accommodations to golf. For information, contact the **South Carolina Division of Tourism** (☞ Visitor Information, *below*).

PACKING FOR THE SOUTH

Much of the South has hot, humid summers and sunny, mild winters. For colder months, pack a lightweight coat, slacks, and sweaters. Keeping summer's humidity in mind, **pack absorbent natural fabrics that breathe**; bring an umbrella, but leave the plastic raincoat at home. You'll want a jacket or sweater for summer evenings and for too-cool air-conditioning. And **don't forget insect repellent.**

Bring an extra pair of eyeglasses or contact lenses in your carry-on luggage, and if you have a health problem, **pack enough medication** to last the entire trip. It's important that you **don't put prescription drugs or valuables in luggage to be checked**: it might go astray. Travelers who suffer allergies

might experience some additional discomfort during spring or fall, when regional pollens could trigger unexpected reactions.

PASSPORTS & VISAS

CANADIANS

A passport is not required to enter the United States.

U.K. CITIZENS

British citizens need a valid passport to enter the United States. If you are staying for fewer than 90 days on vacation, with a return or onward ticket, you probably will not need a visa. However, you will need to fill out the Visa Waiver Form, 1-94W, supplied by the airline.

➤ INFORMATION: **London Passport Office** (☎ 0990/21010) for fees and documentation requirements and to request an emergency passport. **U.S. Embassy Visa Information Line** (☎ 01891/200–290) for U.S. visa information; calls cost 49p per minute or 39p per minute cheap rate. **U.S. Embassy Visa Branch** (✉ 5 Upper Grosvenor St., London W1A 2JB) for U.S. visa information; send a self-addressed, stamped envelope. Write the **U.S. Consulate General** (✉ Queen's House, Queen St., Belfast BTI 6EO) if you live in Northern Ireland.

TELEPHONES

AREA CODES

The area code for Savannah is 912. The area code for

Charleston is 803. In September, 1998, Charleston's area code will change to 843.

CALLING HOME
AT&T, MCI, and Sprint long-distance services make calling home relatively convenient and let you avoid hotel surcharges. Typically you dial an 800 number in the United States.

➤ TO OBTAIN ACCESS CODES: **AT&T USADirect** (☎ 800/874–4000). **MCI Call USA** (☎ 800/444–4444). **Sprint Express** (☎ 800/793–1153).

TRAIN TRAVEL
➤ IN GEORGIA: **Amtrak** serves the state from the Brookwood Station in Atlanta (✉ 1688 Peachtree St., ☎ 404/881–3060 or 800/872–7245). The *Crescent* operates daily to Atlanta from New York; Philadelphia; Washington, DC; Baltimore; Charlotte; and Greenville, and daily from New Orleans to New York through Atlanta. The "Thru-Way" bus service operates daily from Birmingham and Mobile, Alabama, to Atlanta's Brookwood Station. Another bus goes from the train station to Macon.

Amtrak has regular service along the Eastern Seaboard, with daily stops in Savannah (✉ 2611 Seaboard Coastline Dr., ☎ 912/234–2611 or 800/872–7245), where a station is 4 mi southwest of downtown.

➤ IN SOUTH CAROLINA: **Amtrak** (☎ 800/872–7245) stops in Charleston, Camden, Columbia, Denmark, Dillon, Florence, Greenville, Kingstree and Yemassee (near Beaufort).

TRAVEL AGENCIES
A good travel agent puts your needs first. Look for an agency that has been in business at least five years, emphasizes customer service, and has someone on staff who specializes in your destination. In addition, **make sure the agency belongs to the American Society of Travel Agents** (ASTA).

➤ LOCAL AGENT REFERRALS: **American Society of Travel Agents** (ASTA, ☎ 800/965–2782 24-hr hot line, 📠 703/684–8319). In Canada, **Alliance of Canadian Travel Associations** (✉ 1729 Bank St., Suite 201, Ottawa, Ontario K1V 7Z5, ☎ 613/521–0474, 📠 613/521–0805). In Great Britain, **Association of British Travel Agents** (✉ 55–57 Newman St., London W1P 4AH, ☎ 0171/637–2444, 📠 0171/637–0713).

VISITOR INFORMATION
➤ IN GEORGIA: The **Georgia Department of Industry, Trade and Tourism** (✉ Box 1776, Atlanta 30301, ☎ 404/656–3590 or 800/847–4842, 📠 404/651–9063) is the best source for visitor information around the state.

➤ IN SOUTH CAROLINA: **South Carolina Division of Tourism** (✉ 1205

Pendleton St., Columbia 29201, ☎ 803/734–0122 or 800/872–3505) has information about the entire state.

Welcome centers: ⊠ U.S. 17, near Little River; ⊠ I–95, near Dillon, Santee and Lake Marion, and Hardeeville; ⊠ I–77, near Fort Mill; ⊠ I–85, near Blacksburg and Fair Play; ⊠ I–26, near Landrum; ⊠ I–20, at North Augusta; and ⊠ U.S. 301, near Allendale.

➤ IN THE U.K: Georgia (☎ 0121/475–4123, FAX 0121/475–2211); South Carolina (☎ 0181/688–1141, FAX 0181/666–0365).

WHEN TO GO

Spring is probably the most attractive season in this part of the United States. Throughout the region, cherry blossoms are followed by azaleas, dogwood, and camellias from April into May, and by apple blossoms in May. Summer can be hot and humid in many areas, but temperatures will be cooler along the coasts. Folk, craft, art, and music festivals tend to take place in summer, as do sports events. State and local fairs are held mainly in August and September, though there are a few in early July and into October.

CLIMATE

In winter, temperatures generally average in the low 40s inland, in the 60s by the shore. Summer temperatures, modified by mountains in some areas, by water in others, range from the high 70s to the mid-80s, now and then the low 90s.

➤ FORECASTS: **Weather Channel Connection** (☎ 900/932–8437), 95¢ per minute from a Touch-Tone phone.

The following are average daily maximum and minimum temperatures for key Southern cities.

Climate

ATLANTA, GEORGIA

Jan.	52F	11C	May	79F	26C	Sept.	83F	28C
	36	2		61	16		65	18
Feb.	54F	12C	June	86F	30C	Oct.	72F	22C
	38	3		67	19		54	12
Mar.	63F	17C	July	88F	31C	Nov.	61F	16C
	43	6		70	21		43	6
Apr.	72F	22C	Aug.	86F	30C	Dec.	52F	11C
	52	11		70	21		38	3

CHARLESTON, SOUTH CAROLINA

Jan.	59F	15C	May	81F	27C	Sept.	84F	29C
	41	6		64	18		69	21
Feb.	60F	16C	June	86F	30C	Oct.	76F	24C
	43	7		71	22		59	15
Mar.	66F	19C	July	88F	31C	Nov.	67F	19C
	49	9		74	23		49	9
Apr.	73F	23C	Aug.	88F	31C	Dec.	59F	11C
	56	13		73	23		42	6

1 Destination: Savannah and Charleston

SIBLING RIVALRY

ONLY 108 MILES APART along the Atlantic coast, Savannah and Charleston share certain geographical characteristics and historical similarities, and they are both gracious, well-preserved, and small. But although they may be sister cities, they're not identical twins.

Let's first get the clichés over with. Southern hospitality rules in both cities and both have beautiful mansions in a range of architectural styles, horse-drawn carriages clip-clopping on cobblestone streets, lovely gardens, oak trees dripping Spanish moss, and plenty of verandas on which to kick back with a mint julep. Both found wealth in their strategic locations on rivers with quick outlets to the Atlantic; Savannah is still the largest port between Baltimore and New Orleans and draws much of its wealth from port activity and shipbuilding. Both cities were at one time the capitals of their respective states. And both have long military histories. Charleston has Fort Sumter, where the first shots of the Civil War rang out, as well as the Citadel and a navy base. Savannah has Fort Jackson, Confederate headquarters of river batteries, and Fort Pulaski, captured by Union troops in 1862.

And that pesky Sherman ended his march to the sea in Savannah in December 1864—the city was his Christmas present to Lincoln that year.

The first mark of difference between these two cities is, of course, that they're in different states. South Carolina is the smallest southern state while Georgia is the largest state east of the Mississippi. And it might surprise more than a few people that Savannah has a larger population than Charleston and that it throws the second-largest St. Patrick's Day celebration in the States (after New York City). But this does make sense, as Savannah is known to throw a good party. What sets Savannah apart from Charleston most of all is its squares. Savannah has the largest National Historic Landmark District (2½ square miles) in the United States. And oh, those verdant, picture-perfect, made-for-Hollywood squares surrounded by stately, exquisitely kept homes. The moss drips languorously, owners open their homes for tours, and visitors—most of whom have read John Berendt's 1994 best-seller *Midnight in the Garden of Good and Evil*—come. This is Berendt's take on the Savannah–Charleston rivalry:

Savannahians like to talk about Charleston most of all, especially in the presence of a newcomer. They would compare the two cities endlessly. Savannah was the Hostess City; Charleston was the Holy City (because it had a lot of churches). Savannah's street scape was superior to Charleston's but Charleston had finer interiors. Savannah was thoroughly English in style and temperament; Charleston had French and Spanish influences as well as English. Savannah preferred hunting, fishing, and going to parties over intellectual pursuits; in Charleston it was the other way around. Savannah was attractive to tourists; Charleston was overrun by them. On and on. In the minds of most Americans, Savannah and Charleston were sister cities. If so, the sisters were barely on speaking terms. Savannahians rarely went to Charleston, even though it was less than two hours away by car. But then Savannahians rarely went anywhere at all. They could not be bothered. They were content to remain in their isolated city under self-imposed house arrest.

Well, several things have changed since the book's publication, most notably the part about Charleston attracting more visitors. Savannah's profile has been raised pronouncedly by Berendt's book and the movie of the book directed by Clint Eastwood and starring Kevin Spacey and John Cusack. But Charlestonians are taking all this fanfare in stride. They know they are not in danger of complete desertion. They host the wonderful Spoleto Festival of the arts every summer, and they have some of the best restaurants in the South, the most historic inns in the vicinity, and 181 churches. (Lest you think they are teetotalling holy rollers, you should know that it was a Charlestonian who invented Planter's punch.)

Eminently beautiful and strollable Charleston and Savannah give each other a run for their money. (A little sibling rivalry never hurt anyone.)

— Anastasia Mills

NEW AND NOTEWORTHY

Savannah

Savannah continues to attract visitors who have read the best-selling *Midnight in the Garden of Good and Evil* and want to explore the city for themselves. The upcoming movie version of this tale of an antiques dealer accused of murder is fueling interest in the city. The first week in July, Savannah will welcome **America's Sail '98,** a gathering of Tall Ships from around the world. A Parade of Sail will take place in Savannah Harbor, followed by festivities during which some ships will be open to the public. The Tall Ship handicapped race begins at the end of the week and finishes on Long Island, New York four days later.

Charleston

In September 1998, **Around Alone,** the single-handed yacht race around the world (formerly the BOC Challenge) begins in Charleston, as it did in 1994. New Charleston-area **accommodations** will include the Wentworth Mansion, a B&B in an 1886 brick home, and the Inn at Wild Dunes, part of the Wild Dunes resort on the Isle of Palms; these weren't available for inspection at press time. In **restaurant news,** Charleston chef Louis Osteen (formerly of Louis's Charleston Grill) was set to open Louis's Restaurant at 200 Meeting Street. Talented chef Bob Waggoner of Nashville has taken over the Charleston Grill. North Charleston will open the **Carolina Ice Palace,** a twin-rink family entertainment complex with a virtual reality arcade. A major airport expansion will be completed in **Columbia,** the South Carolina state capital, early in the year.

On a practical note, in September 1998 the **area code** for the Charleston area will change from 803 to 843.

WHAT'S WHERE

Georgia is notable for its contrasting landscapes and varied cities and towns, each reflecting its own special Southern charm. The northern part of the state has the Appalachian Mountains and their waterfalls; Dahlonega, the site of the nation's first gold rush; and Alpine Helen, a re-created Bavarian village in the Blue Ridge Mountains. Also in the north is Atlanta, a fast-growing city that serves as a banking center; and Macon, an antebellum town with thousands of cherry trees. If you drive some five hours southeast from Atlanta, you'll reach **Savannah,** which has the nation's largest historic district, filled with restored colonial and 19th-century buildings. From Savannah, the state's 100-mi Atlantic coast runs south to the Florida border. Along this stretch is a string of lush, subtropical barrier islands, the **Golden Isles,** which include the elegant seaside communities of Jekyll, Sea, and St. Simons islands. Farther south is Cumberland Island National Seashore, a sanctuary of marshes, beaches, forests, lakes, and ponds. Southern Georgia consists of black, gator-infested swampland, including the mysterious rivers and lakes of the **Okefenokee.**

South Carolina's scenic Lowcountry shoreline is punctuated by the lively port city of **Charleston,** decked out with fine museums (several in restored antebellum homes) and anchored by the recreational resorts of Myrtle Beach and Hilton Head at either end of the coast. The state capital, Columbia, is set in the fertile interior, and the Blue Ridge

Mountains form the western border of the state. Also to the west are the rolling fields of Thoroughbred Country, noted for top racehorses and sprawling mansions, and Upcountry, at the state's northwestern tip, with incredible mountain scenery and white-water rafting.

GREAT ITINERARIES

The following recommended itineraries, arranged by theme, are offered as a guide to planning individual travel.

Prominent Sites of African-American History

Blacks and whites in South Carolina's Lowcountry have always lived side by side, though, as evidenced by the 1739 Stono Plantation Rebellion and the 1822 Denmark Vesey plot to take over Charleston, not always peaceably. This natural distrust also motivated blacks to develop a lilting dialect called Gullah to communicate exclusively with one another. Historic sites in the Lowcountry recall this unique black experience.

Duration: Two days.

One day: In Charleston, begin with a walking tour of Cabbage Row, home of DuBose Heyward

and setting for his novel *Porgy*. Then see the Emmanuel A.M.E. Church—the place of worship of the South's oldest A.M.E. congregation. Also here is the Old Exchange and Provost Dungeon, site of the city's busiest slave market. The Avery Research Center in the historic district has an archives and museum that document the heritage of Lowcountry blacks.

One day: Travel on to the Beaufort area, where you'll see the Penn Center Historic District and York W. Bailey Cultural Museum on St. Helena Island. This community center consists of 17 buildings on the campus of a school that was established in 1862 for freed slaves. Also in Beaufort County is Daufuskie Island, until recently inhabited exclusively by descendants of slaves.

Prominent Civil War Sites

South Carolina seceded from the Union on December 20, 1860, and the first shot of the war was fired the following April. The following itineraries take in the major sites and sights in South Carolina, Georgia, and Alabama.

Duration: Seven to nine days.

One day: Begin in Charleston, South Carolina, and visit the Fort Sumter National Monument. On April 12, 1861, Confederate General P. G. T. Beauregard ordered the first shot fired, and the bloody four-year struggle began.

Two or three days: Drive the 300 mi south to Atlanta, Georgia. See the Eternal Flame of the Confederacy and visit the Cyclorama, depicting the 1864 Battle of Atlanta. Finally, explore 3,200-acre Stone Mountain Park, where there's a Confederate Memorial carved into the mountain—the world's largest monument.

Two days: From Atlanta, drive 160 mi southwest to Montgomery, Alabama, the Cradle of the Confederacy. Visit the State Capitol, which was the first capitol of the Confederacy, and the First White House of the Confederacy, which was occupied by President Jefferson Davis and his family.

Two or three days: From Montgomery head southwest toward Mobile. Next stop is Fort Morgan, about 20 mi from Gulf Shores. A museum in Fort Morgan describes the dramatic 1864 Battle of Mobile Bay, during which Admiral David Farragut shouted, "Damn the torpedoes! Full speed ahead!"

FODOR'S CHOICE

No two people will agree on what makes a perfect vacation, but it's fun and helpful to know what others think. We hope you'll have a chance to experience some of Fodor's Choices yourself in Sa-

vannah and Charleston. For detailed information about each entry, refer to the appropriate chapter.

Special Moments

★ **Okefenokee National Wildlife Refuge, southeast Georgia.** Savor nature at its most primeval as alligators and frogs bellow their respective mating calls in spring.

★ **Historic District, Savannah, Georgia.** Architecture buffs will have a field day strolling by the hundreds of restored buildings within a 2½-mi-square area.

★ **Cypress Gardens, South Carolina.** A boat tour among the spring blossoms reflecting in the black waters of the gardens is a visual dazzler.

Dining

★ **Elizabeth on 37th, Savannah, Georgia.** In an elegant turn-of-the-century mansion in the city's Victorian district, the emphasis is on seafood enhanced by delicate sauces. *$$$$*

★ **Mrs. Wilkes Dining Room, Savannah, Georgia.** Expect long lines waiting to devour the reasonably priced, well-prepared Southern food, served family-style at big tables. *$*

★ **Magnolias, Charleston, South Carolina.** Lots of Lowcountry dishes and a magnolia theme infuse this refurbished warehouse with Southern charm. *$$–$$$*

Lodging

★ **Cloister Hotel, Sea Island, Georgia.** This famed resort with spacious rooms in a Spanish Mediterranean building has a superb spa and outdoor activities galore—golf, tennis, swimming, skeet shooting, sailing, biking, and fishing. *$$$$*

★ **Kehoe House, Savannah, Georgia.** Elegance, refinement, and Victorian opulence make a stay at this bed-and-breakfast inn a grand experience in every way. *$$$$*

★ **Mulberry Inn, Savannah, Georgia.** This traditional dependable lodging features a number of artistic treasures in its public rooms, including valuable Chinese vases and 18th-century oil paintings. *$$$$*

★ **Charleston Place, Charleston, South Carolina.** The upscale address for Charleston, this full-service hotel is conveniently located in the historic district. *$$$$*

★ **John Rutledge House Inn, Charleston, South Carolina.** One of the newer inns in Charleston, the elegant John Rutledge House is impeccably furnished and maintained. *$$$$*

FESTIVALS AND SEASONAL EVENTS

WINTER

➤ JAN.: Regional **runners race** in the Savannah Marathon and Half Marathon in Savannah, Georgia.

SPRING

➤ MAR.: The Old South comes alive: **Antebellum mansion and garden tours** are given in Charleston and Beaufort, South Carolina. **Spring is celebrated** with Springfest on Hilton Head Island, South Carolina. **St. Patrick's Day** in Savannah is one of the nation's largest celebrations of the day.

➤ MAY: **Spoleto Festival USA,** in Charleston, is one of the world's biggest arts festivals; **Piccolo Spoleto,** running concurrently, showcases local and regional talent. In South Carolina, Beaufort's **Gullah Festival** highlights the fine arts, customs, language, and dress of Lowcountry African-Americans.

SUMMER

➤ JULY: **Independence Day** celebrations are annual traditions around the South, including in Savannah.

➤ AUG.: August **music festivals** include a Beach Music Festival in Jekyll Island, Georgia.

AUTUMN

➤ SEPT.: In Charleston, the daily **Fall Candlelight Tours** of homes and gardens begins mid-month.

Competitions, music, and dancing take place at the **Scottish Games and Highland Gathering** at Boon Hall Plantation. The **Moja Arts Festival** at the end of the month celebrates African American and Caribbean culture with theater, dance, literary readings, lectures and more.

➤ OCT.: Charleston's daily **Fall Candlelight Tours** of homes and gardens continue. Savannah kicks off the month with the German-themed **Oktoberfest** on the Riverfront and finishes it out with the **Tom Turpin Ragtime Festival** and **Haunted Legends Pub Crawl.**

➤ NOV.: Charleston hosts the **Worldfest Charleston International Film Festival,** which is followed mid-month by the **World Finals Rodeo** at North Charleston Coloseum.

2 Savannah

Updated
by Jane F.
Garvey

THE VERY SOUND OF THE NAME Savannah conjures up misty images of mint juleps, live oaks dripping with Spanish moss, handsome mansions, and a somewhat decadent city moving at a lazy Southern pace. Why, you can hardly say "Savannah" without drawling. Well, brace yourself. The mint juleps are there all right, along with the moss and the mansions and the easygoing pace, but this Southern belle rings with surprises. Take, for example, St. Patrick's Day: Why on earth does Savannah, of all places, have a St. Patrick's Day celebration second only to New York's? The greening of Savannah began more than 164 years ago, and nobody seems to know why, although everybody in town talks a blue (green) streak about St. Patrick's Day. Everything turns green on March 17, including the faces of startled visitors when green scrambled eggs and green grits are put before them.

Savannah's beginning was February 12, 1733, when English General James Edward Oglethorpe and 120 colonists arrived at Yamacraw Bluff on the Savannah River to found the 13th and last colony in the New World. As the port city grew, Englishmen, Scottish Highlanders, French Huguenots, Germans, Austrian Salzburgers, Sephardic and Ashkenazic Jews, Moravians, Italians, Swiss, Welsh, Greeks and the Irish all arrived to create what could be called a rich gumbo.

In 1793 Eli Whitney of Connecticut, who was tutoring on a plantation near Savannah, invented a mechanized means of "ginning" seeds from cotton bolls. Cotton soon became king, and Savannah, already a busy seaport, flourished under its reign. Waterfront warehouses were filled with "white gold," and brokers trading in the Savannah Cotton Exchange set world prices. The white gold brought in solid gold, and fine mansions were built in the prospering city.

In 1864 Savannahians surrendered their city to Union General Sherman rather than see it torched. Following World War I and the collapse of the cotton market, the city's economy virtually collapsed, and its historic buildings languished for more than 30 years. Elegant mansions were either razed or allowed to decay, and cobwebs replaced cotton in the dilapidated riverfront warehouses.

But in 1955, Savannah's spirits rose again. News that the exquisite Isaiah Davenport home (⊠ 324 E. State St.) was to be destroyed prompted seven outraged ladies to raise enough money to buy the house. They saved it the day before the wrecking ball was to swing. Thus was born the Historic Savannah Foundation, the organization responsible for the restoration of downtown Savannah, where more than 1,000 restored buildings form the 2½-square-mi Historic District, the nation's largest. Many of these buildings are open to the public during the annual tour of homes, and today Savannah is recognized as one of the top 10 cities in the United States for walking tours.

John Berendt's wildly popular *Midnight in the Garden of Good and Evil,* published in 1994, has dispatched an ever increasing number of new visitors to Savannah. A nonfiction account of a notorious murder that took place in the city in the 1980s, the book brings to life such Savannah sites as Monterey Square, Mercer House, and Bonaventure Cemetery.

Georgia's founder, General James Oglethorpe, designed the original town of Savannah and laid it out in a perfect grid. The Historic District is neatly hemmed in by the Savannah River, Gaston Street, East Street, and Martin Luther King Jr. Boulevard. Streets are arrow-straight, public squares of varying sizes are tucked into the grid at precise intervals, and each block is sliced in half by a lane. Bull Street, anchored on the north by City Hall and the south by Forsyth Park, charges down the center of the grid and lunges around the five public squares that stand in its way.

Numbers in the text correspond to numbers in the margin and on the Savannah Historic District and Midnight in the Garden *maps.*

EXPLORING SAVANNAH

The Historic District

A Good Walk and Drive

Historic Savannah may be covered completely on foot but to save some energy and time, it is best to combine walking with driving. Start at the **Savannah Visitors Center** ①, on Martin Luther King Jr. Boulevard. Housed in the same building, the **Savannah History Museum** ② is an ideal introduction to the city's history. There is public parking next the to center and museum.

Exit the parking lot and turn left (north), walking or driving two short and one very long blocks on Martin Luther King Jr. Boulevard to the **Scarborough House** ③, which contains the Ships of the Sea Museum. Cross Martin Luther King Jr. Boulevard and continue two blocks east on West Congress Street, past Franklin Square to **City Market** ④. Skirting around Franklin Square north on Montgomery Street, go two blocks to West Bay Street, and turn right.

From this point, continue east on West Bay Street four blocks to Bull Street. On your left, you'll see **City Hall** ⑤. Continue east down West Bay Street (which now becomes East Bay Street) to **Factors Walk** ⑥, which lies south of River Street and the Savannah River. If you're driving, leave your car here to continue on foot (be sure to park in long-term parking, as the short-term meters are carefully watched and tickets dispensed expeditiously). Next, visit **Riverfront Plaza** ⑦, which steps down from Factors Walk toward the river, which can only be seen on foot. At this point, if you're driving, you'll probably want to get in your car again to continue the tour.

Return to East Bay Street and head west two long blocks back to Bull Street; turn left going south two blocks on Bull Street to **Johnson Square** ⑧. Twenty-one of Savannah's original 24 squares survive and are restored; they are spaced at four-block intervals in either compass direction.

Walk or drive four blocks south on Bull Street to **Wright Square** ⑨, then turn right (west) two blocks to Telfair Square, where you can stop at the **Telfair Mansion and Art Museum** ⑩. Stroll around Telfair Square, and then continue east on West York Street back toward **Wright Square,** and turn right on Bull Street, walking two blocks south to the **Juliette Gordon Low Birthplace** ⑪. Two more short blocks south from the Low House on Bull Street, you'll reach **Chippewa Square** ⑫. Continue south on Bull Street to **Madison Square** ⑬, where you may stop to take in the

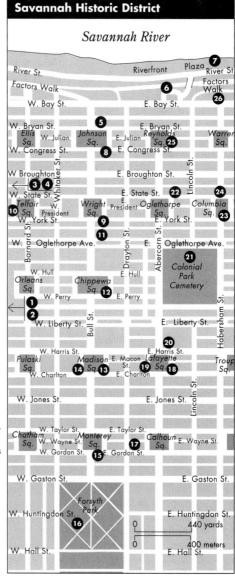

Savannah Historic District

Savannah River

Gothic Revival **Green-Meldrim House** ⑭. Next, walk four blocks south on Bull Street to **Monterey Square** ⑮. Proceed two blocks farther south from Monterey Square to **Forsyth Park** ⑯, the divide between East and West Gaston streets.

From the park, walk east on East Gaston Street and go one block to Abercorn Street; then turn left (north) on Abercorn, to Calhoun Square, and note the **Wesley Monumental Church** ⑰. Continue north on Abercorn eight blocks to **Lafayette Square** ⑱. Walk left a few steps and view the **Andrew Low House** ⑲. Northeast of Lafayette Square looms the **Cathedral of St. John the Baptist** ⑳ on East Harris Street. One block north at the intersection of Abercorn and East Oglethorpe streets is the huge **Colonial Park Cemetery** ㉑. Proceeding two blocks north on Abercorn from the cemetery takes you to Oglethorpe Square; across from the square is the **Owens-Thomas House and Museum** ㉒. From the house, walk east on East President Street two blocks to **Columbia Square** ㉓. Northwest of the square on East State Street stands the **Isaiah Davenport House** ㉔. From here, continue north up Habersham Street two blocks to Warren Square; turn left (west) and go two blocks to **Reynolds Square** ㉕, on Abercorn. Head north on Abercorn to East Bay Street, turn right and then walk one block to **Emmet Park** ㉖, a splendid park to relax in at the end of your tour.

TIMING

This is a long but comfortable walk, as Savannah has no hills or inclines to tax the casual stroller. Allow a full day to see everything along this route, especially to read all the historic markers and explore all the sights thoroughly, including stopping at selected ones for tours within. Driving around the squares can be slow—but the entire drive can be done in two hours, a pace that allows for some stopping along the way. Allow extra time if Riverfront Plaza delights you enough to detain you for a half hour or so.

Sights to See

⑲ **Andrew Low House.** This residence was built in 1848 for Andrew Low, one of Savannah's merchant princes and an investor in the SS *Savannah,* the first steamship to cross the Atlantic Ocean in 1819. The home later belonged to his son William, who married Juliette Gordon. After her husband's death, she founded the Girl Scouts in this house on March

12, 1912. Robert E. Lee and William Thackeray were both entertained here. In addition to its historical significance, the house has some of the best ornamental ironwork in Savannah, fine 19th-century antiques, and stunning silver. ⊠ *329 Abercorn St.,* ☎ *912/233–6854.* ⊠ *$6.* ☉ *Mon.–Wed. and Fri.–Sat. 10:30–4, Sun. noon–4; last tour at 3:30.*

⑳ Cathedral of St. John the Baptist. Soaring like a hymn over the city, the French Gothic–style cathedral, with characteristic pointed arches and free-flowing traceries, is the seat of the Diocese of Savannah. It is the oldest Roman Catholic church in Georgia, having been founded in 1799 by the first French colonists. Fire destroyed the early structures, and the present cathedral dates from 1873. Most of the cathedral's impressive stained-glass windows were made by Austrian glassmakers and imported around the turn of the century. The high altar is of Italian marble, and the Stations of the Cross were imported from Munich. ⊠ *222 E. Harris St.,* ☎ *912/233–4709.*

⑫ Chippewa Square. Daniel Chester French's imposing bronze statue of General James Edward Oglethorpe, founder of Savannah and Georgia, anchors the square. Also note the **Savannah Theatre** on Bull Street, which claims to be the oldest continuously operated theater site in North America.

⑤ City Hall. Built in 1905 on the site of the Old City Exchange (1799–1904), this imposing structure anchors Bay Street. Notice the bench commemorating Oglethorpe's landing on February 12, 1733. ⊠ *1 Bay St.,* ☎ *912/651–6444.* ☉ *Weekdays 8:15–5.*

④ City Market. This popular area encompasses pedestrian-accessed galleries, nightclubs, restaurants, and shops. ⊠ *Between Franklin Sq. and Johnson Sq. on W. Saint Julian St.*

★ ㉑ Colonial Park Cemetery. This park is the final resting place for Savannahians buried here from 1750 to 1853. Shaded pathways lace through the cemetery, and you may want to stroll through and read some of the old inscriptions. There are several historical plaques to look at, one of which marks the grave of Button Gwinnett, a signer of the Declaration of Independence. ⊠ *Oglethorpe and Abercorn Sts.*

㉓ Columbia Square. When Savannah was a walled city (1757–
1790), Bethesda Gate (one of six) was located here. The
square was laid out in 1799.

㉖ Emmet Park. The lovely tree-shaded park is named for
Robert Emmet, a late-18th-century Irish patriot and ora-
tor. ⊠ *Borders Bay St.*

❻ Factors Walk. Cobblestone ramps lead pedestrians down to
River Street. (These are serious cobblestones, and you will
suffer if you wear anything but the most comfortable shoes
you own.) A network of iron walkways connects Bay Street
with the multistoried buildings that rise up from the river level,
and iron stairways descend from Bay Street to Factors Walk.

⓰ Forsyth Park. The park forms the southern anchor of Bull
Street. With 20 luxuriant acres and a glorious white fountain dating from 1858 and restored in 1988, it contains
Confederate and Spanish-American War memorials, and
the Fragrant Garden for the Blind, a project of Savannah
garden clubs. There are tennis courts and a tree-shaded jogging path. The park is often the scene of outdoor plays and
concerts. At the northwest corner of Forsyth Park, in
Hodgson Hall, a 19th-century Italianate–Greek Revival
building, you'll find the **Georgia Historical Society,** which
shows selections from its collection of artifacts and
manuscripts, chiefly concentrating on Georgia history. ⊠
501 Whitaker St., ☎ *912/651–2128.* ☜ *Free.* ☉ *Tues.–
Fri. 10–5, Sat. 9–3.*

★ **⓴ Green-Meldrim House.** Designed by New York architect John
Norris and built in 1852 for cotton merchant Charles
Green, this splendid Gothic Revival mansion cost $90,000
to build—a princely sum back then. The house was bought
in 1892 by Judge Peter Meldrim, whose heirs sold it to **St.
John's Episcopal Church,** for which it is now the working
parish house. General Sherman lived here after taking the
city in 1864. Sitting on **Madison Square,** the mansion is complete with crenelated roof, oriel windows, and an external
gallery with filigreed ironwork. Inside, the mantels are
Carrara marble, the woodwork is carved black walnut, and
the doorknobs and hinges are silver-plated. The house is
furnished with donated 16th-, 17th-, and 18th-century antiques. ⊠ *14 W. Macon St.,* ☎ *912/233–3845.* ☜ *$4.* ☉

Tues. and Thurs.–Sat. 10–4; closed Dec. 15–Jan. 15 and 2 wks before Easter.

★ ㉔ **Isaiah Davenport House.** This residence was the historic Savannah structure whose imminent demolition galvanized the city's residents into action to save their treasured buildings. Semicircular stairs with wrought-iron trim lead to the recessed doorway of the redbrick Federal mansion that master builder Isaiah Davenport built for himself in 1815. Three dormer windows poke through the sloping roof of the stately house, and the interior has polished hardwood floors, fine woodwork and plasterwork, and a soaring elliptical staircase. The furnishings are Hepplewhite, Chippendale, and Sheraton. In the attic, don't miss the collection of antique dolls. ⊠ *324 E. State St.,* ☎ *912/236–8097.* 🖘 *$5.* ⊙ *Daily 10–4.*

❽ **Johnson Square.** The oldest of James Oglethorpe's original 24 squares was laid out in 1733 and named for South Carolina Governor Robert Johnson. A monument marks the grave of Nathanial Greene, a hero of the Revolutionary War. The square was once a popular gathering place, where Savannahians came to welcome President Monroe in 1819, to greet the Marquis de Lafayette in 1825, and to cheer for Georgia's secession in 1861.

⓫ **Juliette Gordon Low Birthplace/Girl Scout National Center.** This majestic Regency town house, attributed to William Jay (built 1818–1821), was designated in 1965 as Savannah's first National Historic Landmark. "Daisy" Low, founder of the Girl Scouts, was born here in 1860, and the house is now owned and operated by the Girl Scouts of America. Mrs. Low's paintings and other artwork are on display in the house, restored to the style of 1886, the year of Mrs. Low's marriage. ⊠ *142 Bull St.,* ☎ *912/233–4501.* 🖘 *$5; discounts for Girl Scouts.* ⊙ *Mon.–Tues. and Thurs.–Sat. 10–4, Sun. 12:30–4:30.*

⓲ **Lafayette Square.** Named for the Marquis de Lafayette, the square contains a graceful three-tier fountain donated by the Georgia chapter of the Colonial Dames of America. ⊠ *Abercorn St. between E. Harris and E. Charlton.*

⓭ **Madison Square.** A statue on the square, laid out in 1839 and named for President James Madison, depicts Sergeant

William Jasper hoisting a flag and is a tribute to his bravery during the Siege of Savannah. Though mortally wounded, Jasper rescued the colors of his regiment in the assault on the British lines. ⌧ *Bull St. between W. Harris and W. Charlton.*

⓯ Monterey Square. Commemorating the victory of General Zachary Taylor's forces in Monterrey, Mexico, in 1846, this is the fifth and southernmost of Bull Street's squares. A monument honors General Casimir Pulaski, the Polish nobleman who lost his life in the Siege of Savannah during the Revolutionary War. **Temple Mickve Israel,** a splendid Gothic Revival synagogue on Monterey Square, is home to the third-oldest Jewish congregation in the United States; its founding members settled in town five months after the establishment of Savannah in 1733. The synagogue's collection includes documents and letters (some from George Washington, James Madison, and Thomas Jefferson) pertaining to early Jewish life in Savannah and Georgia. ⌧ *20 E. Gordon St.,* ☎ *912/233–1547.* ☞ *Free.* ☉ *Weekdays 10–noon and 2–4.*

★ ㉒ Owens-Thomas House and Museum. English architect William Jay's first Regency mansion in Savannah is the city's finest example of that architectural style. Built in 1819, the thoroughly English house was constructed largely with local materials. Of particular note are the curving walls of the house, Greek-inspired ornamental molding, half-moon arches, stained-glass panels, and Duncan Phyfe furniture. You'll find canopied beds, a pianoforte, and displays of ornate silver. From a wrought-iron balcony, in 1825, the Marquis de Lafayette bade a two-hour au revoir to the crowd below. ⌧ *124 Abercorn St.,* ☎ *912/233–9743.* ☞ *$6.* ☉ *Tues.–Sat. 10–4:30, Sun. 2–4:30.*

OFF THE
BEATEN
PATH

RALPH MARK GILBERT CIVIL RIGHTS MUSEUM – In Savannah's stellar historic district, this history museum, opened in 1996, houses a series of 15 exhibits covering segregation from Emancipation through the civil rights movement. The museum has touring exhibitions. ⌧ *460 Martin Luther King Jr. Blvd.,* ☎ *912/231–8900.* ☞ *$4.* ☉ *Mon.–Sat. 9–5, Sun. 1–5.*

㉕ Reynolds Square. John Wesley, who preached in Savannah and wrote the first English hymnal in Savannah in 1736, is remembered here. A monument to the founder of the Methodist Church is shaded by greenery and surrounded by park benches. The **Olde Pink House** (⊠ 23 Abercorn St.), built in 1771, is one of the oldest buildings in town. Now a restaurant (☞ *Dining, below*), the porticoed pink stucco Georgian mansion has been a private home, a bank, and headquarters for a Yankee general during the Civil War.

❼ Riverfront Plaza. Here you can watch a parade of freighters and pug-nosed tugs; youngsters can play in the tugboat-shape sandboxes. River Street is the main venue for many of the city's celebrations, including the First Saturday festivals when flea marketeers, artists, and artisans display their wares, and musicians entertain the crowds.

❷ Savannah History Museum. Housed in a restored railway station, the museum provides an excellent introduction to the city. Exhibits range from old locomotives to a tribute to Savannah-born songwriter Johnny Mercer. The nearby **site of the Siege of Savannah** marks the spot where, in 1779, the Colonial forces, led by Polish Count Casimir Pulaski, laid siege to Savannah in an attempt to retake the city from the Redcoats. They were beaten back, and Pulaski was killed while leading a cavalry charge against the British. ⊠ *303 Martin Luther King Jr. Blvd.,* ☎ *912/238–1779.* ☞ *$3.* ⊙ *Weekdays 8:30–5, weekends 9–5.*

❶ Savannah Visitors Center. Come here for free maps and brochures, lots of friendly advice, and an audiovisual overview of the city. The center is also the starting point for a number of guided tours. The center is in a big 1860 redbrick building with high ceilings and sweeping arches. It was the old Central of Georgia railway station. ⊠ *301 Martin Luther King Jr. Blvd.,* ☎ *912/944–0455.* ⊙ *Weekdays 8:30–5, weekends 9–5.*

❸ Scarborough House. This exuberant Greek Revival mansion, built during the 1819 cotton boom for Savannah merchant Prince William Scarborough, was designed by English architect William Jay. Scarborough was a major investor in the steamship *Savannah*. The house features a Doric portico capped by one of Jay's characteristic half-moon windows. Four massive Doric columns form a peristyle in the atrium entrance hall. The owner of the house, the **Ships of the Sea Museum,** relocated to the Scarborough House in 1996; ship models are on display, including steamships, a nuclear-powered ship (the *Savannah*), China clippers with their sails unfurled, and Columbus's ships. ⊠ *41 Martin Luther King Jr. Blvd.,* ☎ *912/232–1511.* ⧉ *$5.* ☉ *Tues.– Sun. 10–5.*

⓾ Telfair Mansion and Art Museum. The oldest public art museum in the Southeast was designed by William Jay in 1819 for Alexander Telfair, and sits across the street from **Telfair Square.** Within its marbled rooms are American, French, and Dutch Impressionist paintings; German Tonalist paintings; a large collection of works by Kahlil Gibran; plaster casts of the Elgin Marbles, the Venus de Milo, and the Laocoön, among other classical sculptures; and some of the Telfair family furnishings, including a Duncan Phyfe sideboard and Savannah-made silver. ⊠ *121 Barnard St.,* ☎ *912/232–1177.* ⧉ *$5; free Sun.* ☉ *Tues.–Sat. 10–5, Sun. 2–5.*

⓱ Wesley Monumental Church. This Gothic Revival–style church memorializing the founders of Methodism is patterned after Queen's Kirk in Amsterdam. Noted for its magnificent stained-glass windows, the church celebrated a century of service in 1968. In the Wesley Window there are busts of John and Charles Wesley. ⊠ *429 Abercorn St.,* ☎ *912/232–0191.*

⑨ Wright Square. Named for James Wright, Georgia's last Colonial governor, the square has an elaborate monument in its center which honors William Washington Gordon, founder of the Central of Georgia Railroad. A slab of granite from Stone Mountain honors the grave of Tomo-Chi-Chi, the Yamacraw chief who befriended General Oglethorpe and the colonists.

Midnight in the Garden of Good and Evil

Town gossips can give you the best introduction to a city and, as author John Berendt discovered, Savannah's not short on them. In his 1994 best-seller, *Midnight in the Garden of Good and Evil,* Berendt shares the juiciest of tales imparted to him during the eight years he spent here wining and dining with Savannah's high society and dancing with her Grand Empress drag queen, The Lady Chablis, among others. By the time he left, there had been a scandalous homicide and several trials.

Before you set out, find a copy of the book, pour yourself a cool drink, and enter an eccentric world of cutthroat killers and society back stabbers, voodoo witches, and garden-club ladies. Next, slip on a pair of comfortable shoes and head over to the historic district to follow the characters' steps to their homes and haunts. By the end of this walking tour, you'll be hard-pressed to find the line between Berendt's creative nonfiction and Savannah's reality. Note: Unless otherwise indicated, the sights on this tour are not open to the public.

A Good Walk and Drive

Begin at the southwest corner of Monterey Square, site of the **Mercer House** ㉗, whose construction was begun by songwriter Johnny Mercer's great grandfather just before the Civil War. Two blocks south on Bull Street is the **Armstrong House** ㉘, an earlier residence of Jim Williams, the main character in the book. Walk south through Forsyth Park to the corner of West Gaston and Whitaker streets (or, if driving, turn right on East Gaston to West Gaston Street, then left onto Whitaker). The **Forsyth Park Apartments** ㉙, where author John Berendt lived, are on the southwest corner of Forsyth Park. Then, if you're walking, turn back north through the park (and if driving, turn left down Drayton Street at the park's southeast corner, then left onto East Gaston Street). At the midpoint of the park's northern edge, turn north up Bull Street in the direction of Monterey Square. Turn left on West Gordon Street at Bull Street and walk toward the corner of West Gordon and Whitaker, where you'll reach **Serena Dawes's House** ㉚. Next, cross West Gordon Street, walk north on Bull Street in front of Mercer House, cross Wayne Street, and the first house on the left facing Bull at Wayne is **Lee Adler's Home** ㉛, which sits across from Monterey Square's northwest corner. (If you're driving, proceed around Monterey Square to West Taylor Street, and at its intersection with Whitaker Street, take a left and go two blocks to West Gordon. Take a left onto West Gordon; the house is on the right.)

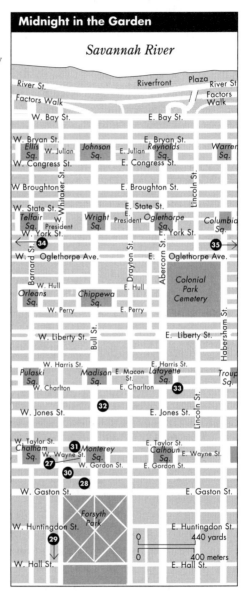

Midnight in the Garden

Continue walking north on Bull Street, and take a right (east) on East Jones Street. **Joe Odom's first house** ㉜ is the third house on the left before Drayton Street. (If you're driving, go around the square again onto Bull Street, and go north on Bull to East Jones Street. Take a right, and the house will be on the left.)

Continue on East Jones Street to Abercorn Street, and turn left (north), walking two blocks on Abercorn to East Charlton Street and the **Hamilton-Turner House** ㉝. Then, swing around Lafayette Square to East Harris Street, and take it about six blocks west to Pulaski Square at Barnard Street; turn right (north) on Barnard through Orleans Square back north to Telfair Square. On foot, you may elect to head west down West York Street on the south side of Telfair Square to find the **Chatham County Courthouse** ㉞, scene of all those trials, two blocks away. Drivers will have to continue around the square to take a left (west) onto West State Street, two blocks from the courthouse. Finally, whether walking or driving, you may conclude the tour by driving east on Liberty Street and Wheaton Street for about 4 mi to Bonaventure Road. Turn left to **Bonaventure Cemetery** ㉟.

TIMING

Allow a leisurely two hours to walk the main points of the tour, plus another hour to visit the cemetery. If driving, this tour is easily accomplished in an hour, but remember to add additional time to meander around Bonaventure Cemetery.

Sights to See

㉘ **Armstrong House.** Jim Williams lived and worked in this residence before purchasing the Mercer House. On a late-afternoon walk past the mansion, Berendt met Mr. Simon Glover, an 86-year-old singer and porter for the law firm of Bouhan, Williams, and Levy, occupants of the building. Glover confided that he earned a weekly $10 for walking one of the firm's former partner's deceased dogs up and down Bull Street. Baffled? So was the author. Behind the house's cast-iron gates are the offices of Frank Siler, Jim Williams's attorney, who doubles as keeper of Uga, the Georgia Bulldog mascot. ✉ *447 Bull St.*

㉟ **Bonaventure Cemetery.** Drive on Wheaton Street east out of downtown to Bonaventure Road. Once the grounds of a magnificent live oak–shaded plantation, whose mansion burned to the ground in the midst of a dinner party, Bonaventure is the final resting place for songwriter Johnny Mercer, poet Conrad Aiken, and also Danny Hansford (Greenwich Cemetery section). While you may be able to find Danny's marker, don't look too hard for the haunting female tombstone figure from the book's cover. Apparently, Berendt fans beat too tough a path to her feet, and she was removed. (Note: Get there before sundown, when it closes.)

34 Chatham County Courthouse. The courthouse was the scene of the three Williams murder trials, which took place over the course of about eight years. An underground tunnel leads from the courthouse to the jail where Williams was held in a specially modified cell that allowed him to conduct his antiques business. ⊠ *133 Montgomery St.*

29 Forsyth Park Apartments. Here was Berendt's second home in Savannah; from his fourth-floor rooms he pieced together the majority of the book. While parking his newly acquired 1973 Pontiac Grand Prix outside these apartments, Berendt met The Lady Chablis coming out of her nearby doctor's office, freshly feminine from a new round of hormone shots. ⊠ *Whitaker and Gwinnett Sts.*

33 Hamilton-Turner House. After one too many of Odom's deals went sour, Mandy left him and took over his third residence, a Second Empire–style mansion dating from 1873. Mandy (or Nancy Hillis, as her driver's license reads) filled it with 17th- and 18th-century antiques; she has since transformed it into a successful museum through which she sometimes leads tour groups. The sturdily elegant towering hulk is at the southeastern corner of Lafayette Square. ⊠ *330 Abercorn St.,* ☎ *912/233–4800.* ☞ *$5.* ☺ *Daily 10–4.*

32 Joe Odom's First House. At this stucco town house, Odom, a combination tax lawyer, real-estate broker, and piano player, played host to a 24-hour stream of visitors. The author met Odom through his fourth fiancée-in-waiting, Mandy Nichols, a former Miss Big Beautiful Woman, who stopped by to borrow ice when their power had been cut off, a frequent occurrence. ⊠ *16 E. Jones St.*

㉛ Lee Adler's Home. Just north of the Mercer House, in half of the double town house facing West Wayne Street, Lee Adler, the adversary of Jim Williams (the main character of the book) runs his business of restoring historic Savannah properties. Adler's howling dogs drove Williams to his pipe organ, where he churned out a deafening version of César Franck's *Pièce Heroique*. Later, Adler stuck reelection signs in his front lawn, showing his support for the District Attorney who prosecuted Williams three times before he was finally found not guilty. ⊠ *425 Bull St.*

㉗ Mercer House. This redbrick Italianate mansion on the southwest corner of Monterey Square became the Taj Mahal of the book's main character, Jim Williams; here he ran a world-class antiques dealership and held *the* Christmas party of the season; here also his sometime house partner Danny Hansford was shot and died. Williams himself died here in 1990, near the very spot where Hansford fell. Today, his sister lives quietly among the remnants of his Fabergé collection and his Joshua Reynolds paintings, in rooms lit by Waterford crystal chandeliers. ⊠ *429 Bull St.*

㉚ Serena Dawes's House. Near the intersection of West Gorden and Bull streets, this house was owned by Helen Driscoll, also known as Serena Dawes. A high-profile beauty in the 1930s and '40s, she married into a Pennsylvania steel family. After her husband accidentally and fatally shot himself in the head, she retired here, in her hometown. Dawes, Berendt writes, "spent most of her day in bed, holding court, drinking martinis and pink ladies, playing with her white toy poodle, Lulu." Chief among Serena's gentlemen callers was Luther Driggers, rumored to possess a poison strong enough to wipe out the entire city. ⊠ *17 W. Gordon St.*

Other Area Attractions

Ebenezer. When the Salzburgers arrived in Savannah in 1734, Oglethorpe sent them up the Savannah River to establish a settlement. The first effort was assailed by disease, and they sought his permission to move to better ground. Not receiving it, they moved anyway and established Ebenezer. There, they engaged in silkworm production and, in 1769, built their Jerusalem Church, which still stands. Following the Revolution, the silkworm operation never resumed, and the town faded into history. Descendants of these original Protestant religious refugees have preserved the church, perhaps Georgia's oldest in continuous use by the same sect, and have assembled a few of the remaining buildings, moving them to this site from other locations. Be sure to follow GA 275 to its end and see Ebenezer Landing, where the Salzburgers came ashore. ⊠ *Ebenezer Rd., Rincon, U.S. 21 to GA 275, Rincon.*

Fort Jackson. About 3½ mi outside Savannah, you'll see a sign for the fort, located on Salter's Island. The Colonial building was purchased in 1808 by the federal government and is the oldest standing fort in Georgia. It was garrisoned in 1812 and was the Confederate headquarters of the river batteries. The brick edifice is surrounded by a tidal moat, and there are 13 exhibit areas. Battle reenactments, blacksmithing demonstrations, and programs of 19th-century music are among the fort's schedule of activities. ⊠ *1 Ft. Jackson Rd.,* ☎ *912/232–3945.* ⊠ *$2.50.* ⊙ *Daily 9–5.*

★ ☾ **Fort Pulaski National Monument.** Just 14 mi east of downtown Savannah, this must-see sight for Civil War buffs was built on Cockspur Island between 1829 and 1847 and named for Casimir Pulaski, a Polish count who was a Revolutionary War hero. Robert E. Lee's first assignment after graduating from West Point was as an engineer here. During the Civil War the fort fell on April 11, 1862, after a mere 30 hours of bombardment by newfangled rifled cannons. The restored fortification, operated by the National Park Service, is complete with moats, drawbridges, massive ramparts, and towering walls. You'll see the entrance on your left just before U.S. 80E reaches Tybee Island. The park has self-guided trails and ample picnic areas. ⊠ *U.S. 80,* ☎ *912/ 786–5787.* ⊠ *$2.* ⊙ *Daily 8:30–5; extended summer hrs.*

King-Tisdell Cottage. Tucked behind a picket fence is this museum dedicated to the preservation of African-American history and culture. The Negro Heritage Trail Tour (☞ *Guided Tours in* Savannah A to Z, *below*) visits this little Victorian house. Broad steps lead to a porch, and dormer windows pop up through a steep roof. The interior is furnished to resemble a middle-class African-American coastal home of the 1890s. To reach the cottage by car, go east on

East Bay Street to Price Street, and turn south (right) on this street; continue for about 30 blocks to East Huntington Street, and take a left (east). The building is in the middle of the block. ⊠ *514 E. Huntingdon St.,* ☎ *912/236–5161.* ☑ *$2.50.* ⊘ *Tues.–Fri. noon–4:30, weekends 1–4.*

Mighty Eighth Air Force Museum. The famous World War II squadron, the Mighty Eighth Air Force, was formed in Savannah in January 1942 and moved to the United Kingdom. Flying borrowed aircraft, it became the largest air force in the history of aviation, with some 200,000 combat crew personnel. Many lost their lives or were interned as prisoners of war. Opened in 1996, a sleek modern building houses memorabilia from the unit's heyday and the era in which it served. ⊠ *I–95 and U.S. 80, 175 Bourne Ave., Exit 18, Pooler,* ☎ *912/748–8888 or 800/421–9428.* ☑ *$7.50.* ⊘ *Daily 10–6.*

Oatland Island Education Center. This 175-acre maritime forest five minutes from downtown is a natural habitat for coastal wildlife, including timber wolves and panthers. ⊠ *711 Sandtown Rd.,* ☎ *912/897–3773.* ☑ *$1 donation requested.* ⊘ *Weekdays 8:30–5; special events and programs Oct.–May, 2nd Sat. of month 11–5.*

Skidaway Marine Science Complex. This center on the grounds of the former Modena Plantation has a 12-panel, 12,000-gallon aquarium with marine and plant life of the continental shelf. Other exhibits highlight coastal archaeology and fossils of the Georgia coast. Nature trails overlook marsh and water. ⊠ *30 Ocean Science Circle, Skidaway Island,* ☎ *912/598–2496.* ☑ *$1.* ⊘ *Weekdays 9–4, Sat. noon–5.*

Tybee Island. Lying 18 mi east of Savannah on the Atlantic Ocean, Tybee has all manner of water and beach activities. Take Victory Drive (U.S. 80), sometimes called Tybee Road, onto the island. There are two historic forts to visit on the way (☞ Fort Jackson and Fort Pulaski National Monument, *above*). "Tybee" is an Indian word meaning salt. The Yamacraw Indians came to the island to hunt and fish, and legend has it that pirates buried their treasure here. The island is about 5 mi long and 2 mi wide, with a plethora of seafood restaurants, chain motels, condos, and shops, most of which sprung up during the 1950s and haven't changed much since. The entire expanse of white sand is divided into a number of public beaches, where visitors shell and crab, play on water slides, charter fishing boats, swim, and build sand castles. Nearby "Little" Tybee Island, actually larger than Tybee Island, is entirely undeveloped, making it ideal for pitching a dome tent and getting away from it all. Contact **Tybee Island Beach Visitor Information** (✉ Box 1628, Savannah 31402, ☎ 800/868–2322).

Tybee Museum and Lighthouse. On the northern end of Tybee Island, across the way from Fort Screven, this museum displays Indian artifacts, pirate pistols, powder flasks, old prints tracing the history of Savannah, and even some sheet music of Johnny Mercer songs. The Civil War Room has old maps and newspaper articles pertaining to Sherman's occupation of Savannah. The 150-ft-high lighthouse across the road is Georgia's oldest and tallest, dating from 1773, with an observation deck 145 ft above the sea. Bright red steps—178 of them—lead to the deck and the awesome Tybee Light. ✉ *30 Meddin Dr.,* ☎ *912/786–4077 museum, 919/786–5801 lighthouse.* 🖾 *Both lighthouse and museum $3.* ☉ *Both summer, Wed.–Mon. 10–6; winter, Mon. and Wed.–Fri. noon–4, weekends 10–4.*

DINING

On a river, 18 mi inland from the Atlantic Ocean, Savannah naturally has excellent seafood restaurants. Locals also have a passion for spicy barbecue. The Historic District yields culinary treasures among its architectural diamonds—especially along River Street. Several of the city's restaurants—such as Elizabeth on 37th, 45 South, the Olde Pink House, and Il Pasticcio—can easily compete with the best of Atlanta's dining establishments. Savannahians also like to drive out to eat in Thunderbolt and on Skidaway, Tybee, and Wilmington islands.

Dress in Savannah—and elsewhere in the state—is casual unless otherwise noted. On the byways of Georgia, barbecue stands and restaurants still cook the whole pig, serving customers its meat pulled off the bone for sandwiches or its tender ribs, both bathed in tangy sauce. Brunswick stew, a hunter's stew, is the standard accompaniment. Some of these places are full-fledged restaurants; others have no place to sit at all. If you're off the beaten path, these establishments offer your best chance for decent food.

CATEGORY	COST*
$$$$	over $50
$$$	$35–$50
$$	$25–$35
$	under $25

per person for a three-course meal, excluding drinks, service, and 6% tax

$$$$ ✕ **Elizabeth on 37th.** Elizabeth Terry is the chef, and in 1995
★   she was named James Beard Best Chef/Southeast. The restaurant is in the city's Victorian District, in an elegant turn-of-the-century mansion with hardwood floors and spacious rooms. Among the seasonal specialties are grouper with sesame seeds, tiny Bluffton oysters with leeks and country ham in the fall and winter, and stuffed Vidalia onions. While the emphasis is on sea creatures served in delicate sauces, there are other excellent offerings, including beef tenderloin, quail, lamb, game, and chicken dishes. The Savannah Cream Cake is a study in layered extravagance. ⊠ *105 E. 37th St.,* ☎ *912/236–5547. Reservations essential. AE, D, DC, MC, V. Closed Sun. No lunch.*

$$$$ ✕ **45 South.** This popular southside eatery is small and
★   stylish, with contemporary decor in lush mauve and green. The ever-changing menu includes seared breast of duck with wild rice, ginger beets, and a Port wine and pear reduction sauce; and grilled ahi tuna with spinach, seared Hudson Valley foie gras, and a truffle vinaigrette. The wine list offers more than a dozen by the glass. ⊠ *20 E. Broad St.,* ☎ *912/ 233–1881. Reservations essential. AE, D, DC, MC, V. Closed Sun. No lunch.*

$$$ ✕ **Olde Pink House.** The brick Georgian mansion was built
★   for James Habersham, one of the wealthiest Americans of his time, in 1771. The elegant tavern, one of Savannah's oldest buildings, has original Georgia pine floors, Venetian chandeliers, and 18th-century English antiques. The owners have introduced Colonial cooking style to the menu where appropriate. Signature dishes are a Colonial version of crisp roast duck with a savory wild-berry compote, and black

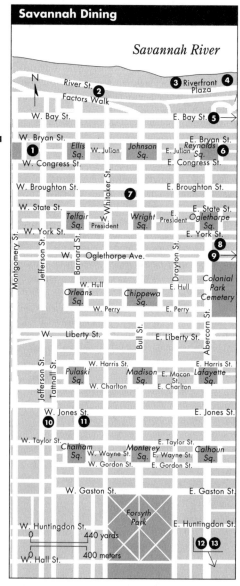

Savannah Dining

Savannah River

grouper stuffed with blue crab. The restaurant has one of the largest wine cellars in the state—fitting, as the Habersham family dominated the Madeira trade for years. ⊠ *23 Abercorn St.,* ☎ *912/232–4286. AE, MC, V. No lunch.*

$$–$$$ ✕ **River House.** This stylish restaurant sits over the spot where the SS *Savannah* set sail for her maiden voyage across the ocean in 1819. The mesquite-grilled entrées, including swordfish topped with vegetables and grouper Florentine, served with creamed spinach and a fresh dill and lemon-butter sauce, are good choices. Entrées are served with freshly baked loaves of sourdough bread, and fish dishes come with homemade angel-hair pasta. The extensive wine list favors California selections. ⊠ *125 W. River St.,* ☎ *912/ 234–1900. AE, D, DC, MC, V.*

$$ ✕ **Bistro Savannah.** Wicker-basket chairs, high ceilings, burnished heart-pine floors, and Savannah gray-brick walls lined with artwork by local artists all contribute to the true bistro atmosphere. Lowcountry dishes form the heart of the inventive menu, such as tasso ham and shrimp on stone-ground grits and pecan-crusted chicken. More modern tastes are represented, too, in such treats as shallot-marinated grilled tuna served with roasted seasonal vegetables. The restaurant is near City Market. ⊠ *309 W. Congress St.,* ☎ *912/233–6266. AE, MC, V. No lunch.*

$$
★ ✕ **Il Pasticcio.** Sicilian Pino Venetico turned this former department store into his dream restaurant. Also a deli, the bistro-style spot gleams with steel, glass, and tile, and is lively with the buzz of a young, hip crowd. The menu changes frequently, but fresh pastas with inventive sauces are a constant. Don't miss the second-floor art gallery. Excellent homemade desserts (a superior tiramisu) and a good wine list make this one worth seeking out. ⊠ *2 E. Broughton St.,* ☎ *912/231– 8888. AE, D, DC, MC, V. Deli closed Sun. No lunch.*

$–$$ 𝍌 **Huey's.** This place right on Riverfront brings the best of Cajun and Creole cooking to the Lowcountry. It's ideal for breakfast, with terrific beignets—those crispy fried doughnuts covered with powdered sugar—hefty egg dishes, pancakes, and waffles. Fairly standard New Orleans–style Southern fare governs lunch and dinner, such as shrimp Creole at lunch and Bayou seafood platter or pasta jambalaya at dinner. ⊠ *115 E. River St.,* ☎ *912/234–7385. Reservations not accepted. AE, D, MC, V.*

$–$$ ✕ **Shrimp Factory.** Like all of Savannah's riverfront restaurants, this was once an old warehouse. Now it's a light and airy place with exposed brick, wood paneling, beamed ceilings, and huge windows that let you gaze at the passing parade of ships. A house specialty is Pine Bark Stew—five native seafoods simmered with potatoes, onions, and herbs. Blackened mahimahi fillet is smothered with herbs and julienned sweet red peppers in butter sauce. Baked deviled crabs are served with chicken-baked rice, and seafood bisque comes with a tiny cruet of sherry. ⊠ *313 E. River St.,* ☎ *912/236–4229. AE, D, DC, MC, V.*

$ ✕ **Crystal Beer Parlor.** This comfortable family tavern is famed for hamburgers, thick-cut french fries, huge onion rings, and frosted mugs of draft beer. The menu also offers fried oyster sandwiches, gumbo, and shrimp salad. ⊠ *301 W. Jones St., at Jefferson St.,* ☎ *912/232–1153. Reservations not accepted. MC, V. Closed Sun.*

$ ✕ **Johnny Harris.** What started as a small roadside stand in 1924 has grown into one of the city's mainstays, with a menu that includes steaks, fried chicken, seafood, and a variety of meats spiced with the restaurant's famous sauce. ⊠ *1651 E. Victory Dr.,* ☎ *912/354–7810. AE, D, DC, MC, V. Closed Sun.*

$ ✕ **Mrs. Wilkes Dining Room.** At breakfast time and noon
★   (no dinner is served), folks line up for a culinary orgy. Charles Kuralt and David Brinkley are among the celebrities who have feasted on the fine Southern food, served family-style at big tables. For breakfast there are eggs, sausage, piping hot biscuits, and grits. At lunch, try fried or roast chicken, collard greens, okra, mashed potatoes, corn bread—the dishes just keep coming. ⊠ *107 W. Jones St.,* ☎ *912/232–5997. Reservations not accepted. No credit cards. Closed weekends. No dinner.*

$ ✕ **Nita's Place.** Opened in 1993 just a half block from the Colonial Cemetery, this little steam-table operation offers nothing in decor. But Juanita Dixon has established a reputation for perfectly prepared down-home Southern cooking; locals and tourists alike come for salmon patties, baked chicken, perfectly cooked okra, outstanding squash casserole, freshly made lemonade—you can see the seeds!—and homemade desserts. The vegetables, always fresh, alone are worth the trip. ☒ *40 Abercorn St.,* ☏ *912/238–8233. Reservations not accepted. MC, V. Closed Sun. No dinner.*

$ 🏚 **Walls'.** Got to have some down-home barbecue with a unique tang and a hint of South Carolina mustard-style sauce? Place your order at the counter and then wait at an orange plastic booth until you're called to pick it up. Serve yourself a drink from the refrigerator case. Basic? Only if you consider heaven basic. Barbecue ribs and sandwiches with sliced meat (get the hot version of the sauce for these), fried or barbecued chicken, exquisite collard greens, and deviled crab are divine. The rib snack makes a perfect nibble in midafternoon following an amble through the historic district. ☒ *515 E. York La. at Price St., between Oglethorpe Ave. and York St.,* ☏ *912/232–9754. Reservations not accepted. No credit cards. Closed Mon. and Tues. No dinner Wed.*

LODGING

While Savannah has its share of chain hotels and motels, the city's most distinctive lodgings are the more than two dozen historic inns, guest houses, and bed-and-breakfasts gracing the Historic District.

If "historic inn" brings to mind images of roughing it in shabbily genteel mansions with slightly antiquated plumbing, you're in for a surprise. Most of the inns are in mansions with the requisite high ceilings, spacious rooms, and ornate carved millwork. Most have canopied, four-poster, or Victorian brass beds. And amid antique surroundings, modern luxury: enormous baths, many with whirlpool baths or hot tubs; film libraries for in-room VCRs; and turndown service with a chocolate, praline, or even a discreet brandy on your nightstand. Continental breakfast and afternoon refreshments are often included in the rate.

CATEGORY	COST*
$$$$	over $100
$$$	$75–$100
$$	$50–$75
$	under $50

All prices are for a standard double room, excluding 13% tax and service.

Inns and Guest Houses

$$$$ 🏨 **Ballastone Inn.** This sumptuous inn occupies a mansion
★   dating from 1838 that once served as a bordello. Each
room has a different decor. Scarborough Fair is a deep
China blue and yellow with two four-poster beds. Mulberry
Tulips has two queen-size antique iron beds. On the garden level, rooms are small and cozy, with exposed brick walls,
beamed ceilings, and, in some cases, windows at eye level
with the lush courtyard. Most rooms have fireplaces, and
three have whirlpool tubs. Guests can exercise for free at
the First City Club nearby. ⊠ *14 E. Oglethorpe Ave.,
31401,* ☏ *912/236–1484 or 800/822–4553,* ℻ *912/236–
4626. 15 rooms, 3 suites. In-room VCRs, concierge. AE,
MC, V.*

$$$$ 🏨 **Eliza Thompson House.** Eliza Thompson was a socially
prominent widow when she built her fine town house
around 1847. Restored and operating as a bed-and-
breakfast in the 1980s, the property declined once more.
But in 1995 Carol and Steve Day purchased the house and
repainted, refinished, and refurnished it in period style.
Continental breakfast and complimentary afternoon wine
and cheese are served on the patio, with its fine Ivan Bailey sculpture. ⊠ *5 W. Jones St., 31401,* ☏ *912/236–3620
or 800/348–9378,* ℻ *912/238–1920. 23 rooms. Concierge.
AE, MC, V.*

$$$$ 🏨 **Foley House Inn.** Two town houses, built 50 years apart,
★   form this elegant bed-and-breakfast inn. Named for an
Irish immigrant who made a fortune in Savannah, the
house was built by his widow for her five grandchildren,
whose parents had died leaving them in her care. Inge and
Mark Moore purchased the inn in 1994 and have completely
renovated it, adding fine antiques and reproductions. Continental breakfast may be served in your room, the lounge,
or outdoors in the courtyard. Afternoon wine is available
for an extra charge. Five rooms have whirlpool tubs. ⊠ *14
W. Hull St., 31401,* ☏ *912/232–6622 or 800/647–3708,*
℻ *912/231–1218. 19 rooms. In-room VCRs, concierge.
AE, MC, V.*

$$$$ 🏨 **Gastonian.** Recently purchased by Decaturite Ann Lan-
★   ders, the mansion was built in 1868, and each of its 10 rooms
and three sumptuous suites is done up in vivid Scalaman-
dre colors. The Caracalla Suite is named for the marble bath

Ballastone Inn, **9**

Days Inn/Days Suites, **1**

DeSoto Hilton, **11**

Eliza Thompson House, **12**

Foley House Inn, **10**

Gastonian, **13**

Hyatt, **2**

Kehoe House, **7**

Mulberry Inn, **6**

Olde Harbour Inn, **3**

Presidents' Quarters, **8**

River Streeet Inn, **4**

Savannah Marriott Riverfront, **5**

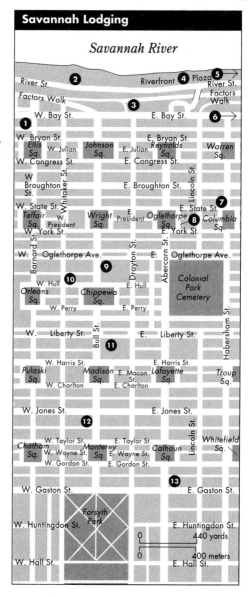

with an 8-ft whirlpool tub. The huge bedroom has a king-size canopy bed, two working fireplaces, and a lounge with a mirrored wet bar. All rooms have working fireplaces and antiques from the Georgian and Regency periods; most have whirlpool tubs or Japanese soak tubs. In the morning, a full breakfast is served in the kitchen or formal dining room—or you can opt for a Continental breakfast in your room. ⊠ *220 E. Gaston St., 31401,* ☎ *912/232–2869 or 800/ 322–6603,* ℻ *912/232–0710. 16 rooms. Outdoor hot tub, concierge. AE, MC, V.*

$$$$ 🏨 **Kehoe House.** A fabulously appointed bed-and-
★   breakfast inn, the Victorian-style Kehoe House is furnished with brass-and-marble chandeliers, a courtyard garden, a music room, and a sense of the luxurious that defines opulence. On the main floor, a double parlor holds two fireplaces and sweeps the eye upward with its 14-ft ceilings. Here, guests enjoy sumptuous breakfasts. Turndown service includes chocolates, a Kehoe House robe, wine, and bottled water. Complimentary visits to the Downtown Athletic Club are included. ⊠ *123 Habersham St., 31401,* ☎ *912/232–1020 or 800/820–1020,* ℻ *912/231–0208. 15 rooms, including 3 at adjacent town house. Concierge, 2 meeting rooms. AE, D, DC, MC, V.*

$$$$ 🏨 **Presidents' Quarters.** Each room in this classic Savan-
★   nah inn is named for an American president. Guests are greeted with wine and fruit in their rooms, and complimentary afternoon tea tempts them with sumptuous cakes. Continental breakfast is served in the rooms, the lobby, or the courtyard. Turndown service includes a glass of port or sherry. The third floor is no-smoking. ⊠ *225 E. President St., 31401,* ☎ *912/233–1600 or 800/233–1776,* ℻ *912/238–0849. 16 rooms. Outdoor hot tub, concierge, parking. AE, D, DC, MC, V.*

$$$–   🏨 **Olde Harbour Inn.** The building dates from 1892, when
$$$$ it was built on the riverfront as an overall factory, but the old inn is actually a thoroughly modern facility. Each suite has a fully equipped kitchen, including dishwasher and detergent. All suites overlook the river and have wall-to-wall carpeting, exposed brick walls painted white, and a four-poster bed. Each evening an ice-cream treat is brought to your room and placed in the freezer. Cereal, fruit, hot muffins and biscuits, juice, tea, and coffee are served in a

cozy breakfast room each morning. ⊠ *508 E. Factors Walk, 31401,* ☎ *912/234–4100 or 800/553–6533,* ⅉ *912/233–5979. 24 suites. Laundry service, concierge, parking. AE, D, DC, MC, V.*

Hotels and Motels

$$$$ 🏨 **DeSoto Hilton.** Three massive chandeliers glisten over the jardinieres and discreetly placed conversation areas of the spacious lobby. The chandeliers are from the historic DeSoto Hotel that stood on this site long ago. Guest rooms are on the cushy side in a burgundy and deep forest green color scheme, with wall-to-wall carpeting, traditional furniture, and king-size or two double beds. (The best view is from the corner king-size rooms.) Suites come with refrigerators upon request. Golf, tennis, and athletic club privileges in the area are available to guests. A major 1997 renovation freshened up the public and private rooms and enhanced the number of suites. ⊠ *15 E. Liberty St., 31401,* ☎ *912/232–9000 or 800/426–8483,* ⅉ *912/231–1633. 237 rooms, 7 suites. Restaurant, lobby lounge, pool, concierge. AE, D, DC, MC. V.*

$$$$ 🏨 **Hyatt.** When this riverfront hotel was built in 1981, preservationists opposed a seven-story modern structure in the historic district. The main architectural features are the towering atrium and a pleasant central lounge, as well as glass elevators. Rooms have modern furnishings, marble baths, and balconies overlooking the atrium and the Savannah River. **MD's Lounge** is the ideal spot to have a drink and watch the river traffic drift by. **Windows,** the hotel's restaurant, is a great spot for Sunday buffet. ⊠ *2 W. Bay St., 31401,* ☎ *912/238–1234 or 800/233–1234,* ⅉ *912/944–3678. 325 rooms, 21 suites. Restaurant, lobby lounge, indoor pool, concierge, business services. AE, D, MC, V.*

$$$$ 🏨 **Mulberry Inn.** This Holiday Inn property is filled with
★ so many objets d'art in the public rooms that the management has obligingly provided a walking tour brochure. Treasures include 18th-century oil paintings. The restaurant is a sophisticated affair, with crystal chandeliers and mauve velvet Regency furniture. More of an inn in style than a hotel, the Mulberry has an elegant lobby with a grand piano. Daily afternoon tea service is offered here. The spacious courtyard is lushly landscaped. The guest rooms are

in a traditional motif; suites have king-size beds and wet bars. ⊠ *601 E. Bay St., 31401,* ☎ *912/238–1200 or 800/ 465–4329,* 𝗙𝗔𝗫 *912/236–2184. 96 rooms, 26 suites. Restaurant, bar, pool, outdoor hot tub. AE, D, DC, MC, V.*

$$$$ 🏨 **River Street Inn.** This elegant hotel offers panoramic views of the Savannah River. Rooms are furnished with antiques and reproductions from the era of King Cotton. Amenities include turndown service. The interior is so lavish, it's difficult to believe it was once a vacant warehouse dating back to 1817. One floor includes charming shops and a New Orleans–style restaurant. Complimentary breakfast is included. ⊠ *115 E. River St., 31401,* ☎ *912/234– 6400 or 800/253–4229,* 𝗙𝗔𝗫 *912/234–1478. 44 rooms. 3 restaurants, 3 bars, concierge, business services. AE, DC, MC, V.*

$$$$ 🏨 **Savannah Marriott Riverfront.** In the Historic District, the eight-story property with rounded balconies facing the river occupies a choice spot, adjacent to River Street and Factors Walk. ⊠ *100 Gen. McIntosh Blvd., 31401,* ☎ *912/ 233–7722 or 800/228–9290,* 𝗙𝗔𝗫 *912/233–3765. 337 rooms, 46 suites. 2 restaurants, lobby lounge, indoor-outdoor pools, hot tub, health club. AE, D, DC, MC, V.*

$$$ 🏨 **Days Inn/Days Suites.** This downtown hotel is in the Historic District near the City Market, only a block off River Street. Its compact rooms have modular furnishings and most amenities. Interior corridors and an adjacent parking garage minimize its motel qualities. Guests have access to a nearby health club. ⊠ *201 W. Bay St., 31401,* ☎ *912/236–4440 or 800/325–2525. 196 rooms, 57 suites. Restaurant, pool. AE, D, DC, MC, V.*

NIGHTLIFE AND THE ARTS

Savannah's nightlife is a reflection of the city's laid-back, easygoing personality. Some clubs feature live reggae, hard rock, and other contemporary music, but most stay with traditional blues, jazz, and piano-bar vocalists. After-dark merrymakers usually head for watering holes on Riverfront Plaza or the south side.

Bars and Nightclubs

Bar Bar (✉ 312 W. Saint Julian St., ☎ 912/231–1910), a neighborhood hangout, has pool tables, games, and a varied beer selection; the place is popular with locals.

Club One (✉ 1 Jefferson St., ☎ 912/232–0200), a gay bar, is where The Lady Chablis (☞ *Midnight in the Garden of Good and Evil, above*) still bumps and grinds her way down the catwalk, lip-syncing disco tunes in a shimmer of sequin and satin gowns; admission is $5.

Kevin Barry's Irish Pub (✉ 117 W. River St., ☎ 912/233–9626) has a friendly atmosphere and traditional Irish music; it's *the* place to be on St. Patrick's Day. The rest of the year there's a mixed bag of tourists and locals, young and old.

Malone's (✉ 27 Barnard St., ☎ 912/234–3059 or 912/237–9862), a sports bar, has 13 TV screens and monitors. Pool tables and a bar are downstairs. On the third level a dance floor with live entertainment attracts another crowd.

Velvet Elvis (✉ 127 W. Congress St., ☎ 912/236–0665) has a selection of music (modest cover) ranging from punk to jazz.

The Zoo (✉ 121 W. Congress St., ☎ 912/236–6266) is a mix of entertainments: four levels, with industrial and techno music on one; live entertainment on another; Top 40 and dance music on a third; and in the basement, pool tables and video screens.

Jazz and Blues Clubs

Bayou Café and Blues Bar (✉ 14 N. Abercorn St., at River St., ☎ 912/233–6411) has acoustic music during the week, while on the weekend the Bayou Blues Band plays numbers by the Allman Brothers and Eric Clapton. The food has a definite Cajun tone.

Cafe Loco (✉ 1 Old Hwy. 80, Tybee Island, ☎ 912/786–7810), just a few miles outside Savannah on Lazaretto Creek, showcases local blues and acoustic acts on its deck. The Healers, a pure blues outfit, is probably the bar's most popular band. Buffalo shrimp, Lowcountry boil, and seafood and Caribbean-accented chicken specials make great accompaniments to the music.

Crossroads (✉ 219 W. Saint Julian St., ☎ 912/234–5438), Savannah's sole blues nightclub, features live performances by local and national talent Monday through Saturday.

Hard Hearted Hannah's East (✉ 20 E. Broad St., ☎ 912/233–2225) showcases Emma Kelly, the undisputed "Lady of 6,000 Songs," who performs Tuesday through Saturday.

OUTDOOR ACTIVITIES AND SPORTS

Boating

Lake Mayer (✉ Lake Mayer Park, Sallie Mood Dr. and Montgomery Crossroads Dr., ☎ 912/652–6780) has paddle boats rented by the facility, sailing (there's a sailing center), and canoeing (the Red Cross teaches classes).

Saltwater Charters (✉ 111 Wickersham Dr., ☎ 912/598–1814) provides packages ranging from two-hour sightseeing tours to 13-hour deep-sea fishing expeditions. Water taxis to the Barrier Islands are also available.

Public boat ramps are found at **Bell's Landing** (✉ Apache Ave. off Abercorn St.) on the Forest River, **Islands Expressway** (✉ Islands Expressway adjacent to Frank W. Spencer Park) on the Wilmington River, and **Savannah Marina** on the Wilmington River in the town of Thunderbolt.

Golf

Bacon Park (✉ 1 Shorty Cooper Dr., ☎ 912/354–2625) is a public course with 27 holes.

Mary Calder (✉ W. Lathrop Ave., ☎ 912/238–7100) has nine holes.

Henderson Golf Club (✉ 1 Al Henderson Dr., at I–95 and GA 204, [Exit 16], ☎ 912/920–4653) is an 18-hole course about 15 mi from downtown Savannah.

Health Clubs

Jewish Educational Alliance (⊠ 5111 Abercorn St., ☎ 912/ 355–8111) has racquetball courts, a gymnasium, weight room, sauna, whirlpool, outdoor Olympic-size pool, and aerobic dance classes. Open to members of Jewish centers. Guest fees are $10 for the first visit, then $8 per additional visit.

Savannah Downtown Athletic Club (⊠ 7 E. Congress St., ☎ 912/236–4874) offers Lifecycles, StairMasters, Body Master, Nautilus and free-weight equipment, sauna, swimming pool, aerobics, tanning beds, and tae kwon do classes. Guest fees are $7 daily, $25 weekly, and $50 monthly.

YMCA Family Center (⊠ 6400 Habersham St., ☎ 912/ 354–6223) has a gymnasium, aerobics, racquetball, and pool. The guest fee is $5.

Jogging and Running

Low-lying coastal terrain is ideal for jogging.

Forsyth Park (⊠ Bull St. between Whitaker and Drayton Sts.), which is flat as a benne seed wafer, is an especially pleasant environment for walking, jogging, or running.

Tybee Island (☞ *above*) has a white-sand beach that is hard packed and relatively debris free, making it a favorite with runners.

For **suburban jogging trails,** head for **Daffin Park** (⊠ 1500 E. Victory Dr.) with level sidewalks available during daylight hours and **Lake Mayer Park** (⊠ Montgomery Crossroads Rd. at Sallie Mood Dr.) with a mile and a half of level asphalt available 24 hours a day.

Tennis

Bacon Park (⊠ 6262 Skidaway Rd., ☎ 912/351–3850) has 16 lighted asphalt courts.

Forsyth Park (⊠ Drayton St. and Park Ave., ☎ 912/351– 3850) contains four lighted courts available until about 10 PM.

Lake Mayer Park (⊠ Montgomery Crossroads Rd. and Sallie Mood Dr., ☎ 912/652–6780) has eight asphalt lighted courts.

SHOPPING

Find your own Lowcountry treasures among a bevy of handcrafted wares—handmade quilts and baskets; wreaths made from Chinese tallow trees and Spanish moss; preserves, jams, and jellies. The favorite Savannah snack, and a popular gift item, is the benne wafer. It's about the size of a quarter and comes in a variety of flavors.

Shopping Districts

City Market, on West Saint Julian Street, between Ellis and Franklin squares, has sidewalk cafés, jazz haunts, shops, and art galleries.

Riverfront Plaza/River Street is nine blocks of shops housed in the renovated waterfront warehouses, where you can find everything from popcorn to pottery.

Oglethorpe Mall (⊠ 7804 Abercorn Extension, ☎ 912/354–7038) has four department stores (Sears, JCPenney, Belks, Steinmart, and Rich's) and more than 140 specialty shops and restaurants.

Savannah Festival Factory Stores (⊠ 11 Gateway Blvd. S, I–95, Exit 16, ☎ 912/925–3089) sells manufacturers' merchandise at 25%–75% off retail.

Savannah Mall (⊠ 14045 Abercorn St., at Rio Rd., just off I–95, ☎ 912/927–7467) has four major stores (JB White, Belk, Parisian, and Montgomery Ward), along with more than 100 specialty shops and restaurants. Kids delight in its old-fashioned carousel.

Specialty Shops

Antiques

Arthur Smith Antiques (⊠ 1 W. Jones St., ☎ 912/236–9701) has four floors showcasing 18th- and 19th-century European furniture, porcelain, rugs, and paintings.

Claire West Fine Linen and Antiques (✉ 411–413 Whitaker St., ☎ 912/236–8163) fills two buildings with fine European linens, antiques, prints, infants' christening gowns and receiving blankets, engravings, and old and new decorative tabletop objects.

Art Galleries

Compass Prints, Inc./Ray Ellis Gallery (✉ 205 W. Congress St., ☎ 912/234–3537) sells original artwork, prints, and books by internationally acclaimed artist Ray Ellis.

Gallery Espresso (✉ 6 E. Liberty St., ☎ 912/233–5348) has great coffee and a new show every two weeks focusing on work by local artists. A true coffee house, it's open until the wee hours.

Gallery 209 (✉ 209 E. River St., ☎ 912/236–4583) is a co-op gallery, with paintings, watercolors, pottery, jewelry, batik, stained glass, weavings, and sculpture by local artists.

Off the Wall (✉ 412 Whitaker St., ☎ 912/233–8840) exhibits artists from the region, the nation, and the world, rather than from Savannah.

Southern Images (✉ 132 E. Oglethorpe Ave., ☎ 912/234–6449) displays the work of Jack Leigh, whose photograph of Bonaventure Cemetery graces the cover of *Midnight in the Garden of Good and Evil.*

Savannah College of Art and Design (✉ 342 Bull St., ☎ 912/238–2480), a privately owned school, has restored at least 40 historic buildings in the city, some of them housing galleries. Work by faculty and students is often for sale. Stop by **Exhibit A, Pinnacle Gallery,** and the **West Bank Gallery,** but also ask about other student galleries. **Garden for the Arts,** developed on a vacant lot next door to the West Bank Gallery, is a collaboration between the college's architecture and foundation departments. It presents rotating exhibitions by faculty and visiting artists.

Benne Wafers

Byrd Cookie Company (✉ 6700 Waters Ave., ☎ 912/355–1716), founded in 1924, is the best place to get the popular cookies that are also sold in numerous gift shops around town.

Country Crafts
Charlotte's Corner (✉ 1 W. Liberty St., ☎ 912/233–8061) carries expensive and moderately priced Savannah souvenirs, children's clothes and toys, and beach wear.

Georgia Gifts (✉ 217 W. Saint Julian St., ☎ 912/236–1220) is the place to find Georgia-made country crafts and such products as jams, jellies, and preserves.

SAVANNAH A TO Z

Arriving and Departing

By Bus
Greyhound/Trailways (✉ 610 W. Oglethorpe Ave., ☎ 912/232–2135 or 800/231–2222).

By Car
I–95 slices north–south along the Eastern Seaboard, intersecting 10 mi west of town with east–west I–16, which dead-ends in downtown Savannah. U.S. 17, the Coastal Highway, also runs north–south through town. U.S. 80, which connects the Atlantic to the Pacific, is another east–west route through Savannah.

By Plane
Savannah International Airport (☎ 912/964–0514), 18 mi west of downtown, is served by Delta, US Airways, and ValuJet for domestic flights. Despite the name, international flights are nonexistent. The foreign trade zone, a locus for importing, is responsible for the "international" aspect.

Vans operated by **McCall's Limousine Service** (☎ 912/966–5364 or 800/673–9365) leave the airport daily for downtown locations. The trip takes 15 minutes, and the one-way fare is $15 for one person; $25 round-trip for one person; two-person rate is $10 per person one way. Routes can include other destinations in addition to downtown. Advance reservation is required.

Taxi fare from the airport to downtown is $18 for one person, $5 for each additional person.

By car, take I–95 south to I–16 east into downtown Savannah.

By Train

Amtrak has regular service along the Eastern Seaboard, with daily stops in Savannah. The Amtrak station (⊠ 2611 Seaboard Coastline Dr., ☎ 912/234–2611 or 800/872–7245) is 4 mi southwest of downtown. Cab fare into the city is $5–$10, depending on the number of passengers.

Getting Around

Despite its size, much of downtown Historic District can easily be explored on foot. Its grid shape makes getting around a breeze, and you'll find any number of places to stop and rest.

By Bus

Chatham Area Transit (CAT; ☎ 912/233–5767) operates buses in Savannah and Chatham County Monday–Saturday from 6 AM to midnight, Sunday 7 to 7. Some lines may stop running earlier or may not run on Sunday. The CAT Shuttle operates throughout the Historic District; 50¢ one way or $1.50 all-day pass. Buses require $1.20 in exact change, and 5¢ extra for a transfer.

By Taxi

Adam Cab Co. (☎ 912/927–7466) is a reliable, 24-hour taxi service. Calling ahead for reservations could yield a discount. Taxis start at 60¢ and cost $1.20 for each mile.

Contacts and Resources

Emergencies

Dial 911 for **police** and **ambulance** in an emergency.

Guided Tours

Carriage Tours of Savannah (⊠ 10 Warner St., ☎ 912/236–6756 or 800/442–5933) takes you through the Historic District by day or by night at a 19th-century clip-clop pace, with coachmen spinning tales and telling ghost stories along the way. A romantic evening champagne tour in a private carriage will set you back $60, and, although champagne can no longer be included in the cost, guests may bring whatever refreshment they wish; regular tours are a more modest $13. Midnight tours are $15.

Gray Line (⊠ 215 W. Boundary St., 31401, ☎ 912/234–8687) conducts a three-hour tour to Isle of Hope and the Lowcountry, including Thunderbolt (a shrimping community) and Wormsloe Plantation Site. Options include walking tours, minibus tours, and trolley tours. Cost ranges from $13 to $23.

Historic Savannah Foundation (⊠ 212 W. Broughton St., 31401, ☎ 912/234–4088 or 800/627–5030), a preservation organization, leads three-hour excursions to the fishing village of Thunderbolt; the Isle of Hope, with stately mansions lining Bluff Drive; the much-photographed Bonaventure Cemetery on the banks of the Wilmington River; and Wormsloe Plantation Site, with its mile-long avenue of arching oaks. The cost depends on the number of people on tour; it costs $15 per person for a minimum of four persons, but private tours may be arranged, with prices beginning at $40 per hour.

Old Town Trolley Tours (☎ 912/233–0083) has narrated 90-minute tours traversing the Historic District, with on-and-off privileges. Trolleys come by 11 designated stops every half hour 9–4:30; cost is $15.

SPECIAL-INTEREST TOURS

Beach Institute African American Cultural Center (⊠ 502 E. Harris St., ☎ 912/234–8000), the first private school built (1867) for African-American children in Savannah after emancipation, is headquarters for the **Negro Heritage Trail Tour.** A knowledgeable guide traces the city's more than 250 years of black history. Tours begin at the Savannah Visitors Center (☞ The Historic District, *above*). Tours are at 1 PM and 3 PM and cost $12.

Garden Club of Savannah (⊠ Box 13892, 31416, ☎ 912/238–0248) takes you during the spring to selected private gardens tucked behind old brick walls and wrought-iron gates.

A Ghost Talk Ghost Walk Tour (⊠ 127 E. Congress St., ☎ 912/233–3896) should send chills down your spine during an easy 1-mi jaunt through the Old Colonial City.

Tours, lasting an hour and a half, leave from Reynolds Square (⊠ Congress and Abercorn Sts.) at the John Wesley Memorial, in the middle of the square. Call for dates, times, and reservations; cost is $10.

Square Routes (⊠ 60 E. Broad St., Suite 11, ☎ 912/232–6866 or 800/868–6867) provides customized strolls and private driving tours that wend through the Historic District and other parts of the Lowcountry. In-town tours focus on the city's architecture and gardens, and specialized tours include the Midnight in the Garden of Good and Evil walk based on the best-seller. Tours usually last two hours and cost from $15 to $25.

Hospitals

The following area hospitals have 24-hour emergency rooms: **Candler Hospital** (⊠ 5353 Reynolds St., ☎ 912/354–9211). **Memorial Medical Center** (⊠ 4700 Waters Ave., ☎ 912/350–8000).

24-Hour Pharmacy

Revco Drug Center (⊠ Medical Arts Shopping Center, 4725 Waters Ave., ☎ 912/355–7111).

Visitor Information

Savannah Area Convention & Visitor's Bureau (⊠ 222 W. Oglethorpe Ave., 31401, ☎ 912/944–0456 or 800/444–2427, FAX 912/944–0468) can provide maps and brochures about Savannah.

3 The Golden Isles and the Okefenokee

JEKYLL, ST. SIMONS, AND SEA ISLANDS

THE GOLDEN ISLES ARE A STRING of lush, subtropical barrier islands meandering lazily down Georgia's Atlantic coast from Savannah to the Florida border. They have a long history of human habitation; Native American relics have been found on these islands that date from about 2500 BC. According to legend, the Indian nations agreed that no wars would be fought there and that tribal members would visit only in a spirit of friendship. In a similar spirit today, all Georgia beaches are in the public domain.

Each Golden Isle has a distinctive personality, shaped by its history and ecology. Three of them—Jekyll Island, Sea Island, and St. Simons Island—are connected to the mainland by bridges in the vicinity of Brunswick; these are the only ones accessible by automobile. The Cumberland Island National Seashore is accessible by ferry from St. Marys. Little St. Simons Island, a privately owned retreat with guest accommodations, is reached by a private launch from St. Simons. About 50 mi inland is the Okefenokee Swamp National Wildlife Refuge, which has a character all its own.

Numbers in the margin correspond to points of interest on the Golden Isles map.

Cumberland Island

❶ *100 mi from Savannah to St. Marys via I–95, 45 mins by ferry from St. Marys.*

The largest, most southerly, and most accessible of Georgia's primitive coastal islands is Cumberland, a 16- by 3-mi sanctuary of marshes, dunes, beaches, forests, lakes and ponds, estuaries, and inlets. Waterways are home to 'gators, sea turtles, otters, snowy egrets, great blue herons, ibis, wood storks, and more than 300 other species of birds. In the forests are armadillos, wild horses, deer, raccoons, and an assortment of reptiles.

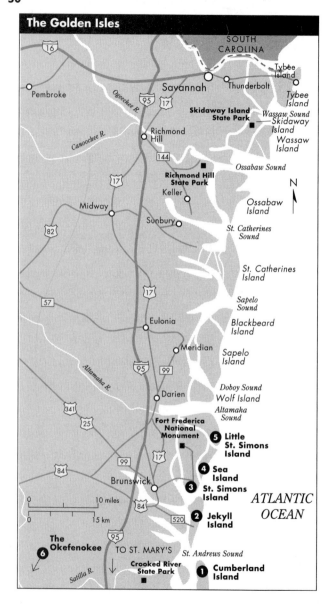

The Golden Isles

SOUTH CAROLINA

16

Pembroke

Savannah Thunderbolt

Tybee Island

95 17

Ogeechee R.

Tybee Island

Skidaway Island State Park

Wassaw Sound

Skidaway Island

Canoochee R.

Richmond Hill

Wassaw Island

144

Ossabaw Sound

17

Richmond Hill State Park

Keller

N

82

Midway

Sunbury

Ossabaw Island

57

17

St. Catherines Sound

St. Catherines Island

Sapelo Sound

Eulonia

Blackbeard Island

Meridian

Sapelo Island

Altamaha R.

95 99

Doboy Sound

Wolf Island

Darien

Altamaha Sound

341

25

Fort Frederica National Monument

5 Little St. Simons Island

99 17

4 Sea Island

84

3 St. Simons Island

Brunswick

ATLANTIC OCEAN

2 Jekyll Island

0 — 10 miles

0 — 15 km

84

520

95

The Okefenokee

TO ST. MARY'S

St. Andrews Sound

6

Crooked River State Park

1 Cumberland Island

Satilla R.

After the ancient Guale Indians came 16th-century Spanish missionaries, 18th-century English soldiers, and 19th-century planters. During the 1880s, the Thomas Carnegie family of Pittsburgh built several lavish homes here, but the island remained largely as nature created it. In the early 1970s, the federal government established the **Cumberland Island National Seashore** and opened this natural treasure to the public. There is no transportation on the island itself, and the only public access to the island is on the *Cumberland Queen,* a reservations-only, 146-passenger ferry based near the National Park Service Information Center at St. Marys. Ferry bookings are heavy in summer, but cancellations and no-shows often make last-minute space available. Reservations may be made as early as 11 months in advance. ⊠ *Cumberland Island National Seashore, Box 806, 31558,* ☎ *912/882–4335,* 🖷 *912/673–7747.* 🎟 *Round-trip $10.07.* ☉ *Mid-May–Sept., ferry departure from St. Marys daily at 9 AM and 11:45 AM, from Cumberland at 10:15 AM and 4:45 PM. No ferry service Tues.–Wed. Oct.–May 14.*

From the Park Service docks at the island's southern end, you can follow wooded nature trails, swim and sun on 18 mi of undeveloped beaches, go fishing and bird-watching, and view the ruins of Carnegie's great estate, **Dungeness.** You can also join history and nature walks led by Park Service rangers. Bear in mind that summers are hot and humid, and that you must bring your own food, soft drinks, sunscreen, and a reliable insect repellent. All trash must be transported back to the mainland by campers and picnickers. Nothing can be purchased on the island.

Dining and Lodging

MAINLAND

$$ ✕ **Seagle's Waterfront Cafe.** The Riverview Hotel, a small seaside lodging, hosts an interesting restaurant that has been recently upgraded, renovated, and converted to a fine dining establishment. Along with renovation came a new menu and more elegant service. Rock shrimp, the local delicacy, comes blackened, fried, steamed, grilled, or broiled. Pecan-crusted grouper fillets in coconut rum sauce and topped with rock shrimp is a weekend special. ⊠ *105 Osborne St., St. Marys,* ☎ *912/882–4187. AE, D, DC, MC, V. Closed Sun.–Mon. No lunch.*

$$ 🏨 **Spencer House Inn.** This comfortable Victorian-style inn dates from 1872. Perfect for walking historic St. Marys and visiting the waterfront, the inn is also handy for boarding the ferry to Cumberland Island. A hefty breakfast is included in the rate. This is a good selection for anyone needing wheelchair access, as there is an elevator. ✉ *101 E. Bryant St., St. Marys 31558,* ☎ *912/882–1872,* 🆔 *912/882–9427. 14 rooms. AE, D, MC, V.*

ISLAND

$$$$ ✕🏨 **Greyfield Inn.** Cumberland Island's only accommodations are in a turn-of-the-century Carnegie family home. Greyfield's public areas are filled with family mementos, furnishings, and portraits (you may feel as though you've stepped into one of Agatha Christie's mysterious Cornwall manors). Prices include all meals, transportation, tours led by a naturalist, and bike rentals. ✉ *Box 900 Fernandina Beach, FL 32035,* ☎ *904/261–6408. 13 rooms. MC, V.*

$ 🛖 **Sea Camp.** A five-minute walk from the *Cumberland Queen* dock, with rest rooms and showers adjacent to campsites, Sea Camp is the ideal spot for novice campers ($8 per person per day). The beach is just beyond the dunes. Experienced campers can hike 3–10 mi to several areas where cold-water spigots are the only amenities.

Jekyll Island

❷ *90 mi from Savannah, 10 mi from Brunswick.*

For 56 winters, between 1886 and 1942, America's rich and famous faithfully came south to Jekyll Island. Through the Gilded Age, the Great War, the Roaring '20s, and the Great Depression, Vanderbilts and Rockefellers, Morgans and Astors, Macys, Pulitzers, and Goodyears shuttered their 5th Avenue castles and retreated to the serenity of their wild Georgia island. There they built elegant "cottages," played golf and tennis, and socialized. Early in World War II, the millionaires departed for the last time. In 1947 the state of Georgia purchased the entire island for the bargain price of $675,000.

Jekyll Island Welcome Center offers tram tours of the Jekyll Island National Historic Landmark District. Tours originate at the Historic District Visitors Center on Stable Road and include several restored buildings in the 240-acre historic district. Faith Chapel, illuminated by Tiffany stained-glass windows, is open for meditation Sunday–Friday 2–4. ⌧ *I–95 to Exit 6, Box 13186, Jekyll Island 31527,* ☎ *912/635–3636 or 800/841–6586,* ⅋⅋ *912/635–4004.* ▱ *$10.* ☉ *Daily 9:30–4, tours daily 10–3.*

Jekyll Island is still a 7½-mi playground, but no longer restricted to the rich and famous. The golf, tennis, fishing, biking, jogging, water park, and picnic grounds are open to all. One side of the island is lined by nearly 10 mi of hard-packed Atlantic beaches; the other by the Intracoastal Waterway and picturesque salt marshes. Deer and wild turkeys inhabit interior forests of pine, magnolia, and moss-veiled live oaks. Egrets, pelicans, herons, and sandpipers skim the gentle surf. Jekyll's clean, mostly uncommercialized public beaches are free and open year-round. Bathhouses with rest rooms, changing areas, and showers are open at regular intervals along the beach. Beachwear, suntan lotion, rafts, snacks, and drinks are available at the **Jekyll Shopping Center,** facing the beach at Beachview Drive.

Dining and Lodging

$$$ ✕ **Grand Dining Room.** In the Jekyll Island Club Hotel the dining room sparkles with silver and crystal. Lowcountry cuisine is the culinary focus, with shrimp, fish, veal, Georgia quail, and lamb. Much of the raw material comes from local sources. California wines dominate the wine list, with a few offerings by the glass. The restaurant has its own label Pinot Noir and Chardonnay, made by Mountain View Vineyards. ⌧ *371 Riverview Dr.,* ☎ *912/635–2600, ext. 1002. Reservations essential. Jacket required at dinner. AE, D, DC, MC, V.*

$$$– ▥ **Jekyll Inn.** On a landscaped 15-acre site, these oceanfront
$$$$ units, the largest facility on the island, recently underwent an extensive renovation. Rooms were redecorated with new lighting and carpeting. Units include some villas with kitchenettes. ⌧ *975 N. Beachview Dr., Jekyll Island 31527,* ☎ *912/635–2531 or 800/736–1046. 264 units. Restaurant, pool, bicycles, playground. AE, D, DC, MC, V.*

$$$–   🏨 **Jekyll Island Club Hotel.** Built in 1886, the four-story club-
$$$$ house with wraparound verandas and Queen Anne–style
towers and turrets once served as the winter hunting retreat
for wealthy financiers. In 1985 a group of Georgia busi-
nessmen spent $17 million restoring it. The guest rooms
and suites are custom-decorated with mahogany beds, ar-
moires, and plush sofas and chairs. Some have flowery
views of the Intracoastal Waterway, Jekyll River, and the
hotel's croquet lawn. The nearby Sans Souci Apartments,
built in 1896 by William Rockefeller, have been converted
into spacious guest rooms. The island itself has 22 mi of
bicycle trails, and the hotel operates a free shuttle to area
beaches. ⊠ *371 Riverview Dr., Jekyll Island 31527,* ☎ *912/
635–2600 or 800/535–9547,* ℻ *912/635–2818. 134
units. 2 restaurants, pool, 9 tennis courts, croquet, bicy-
cles. AE, D, DC, MC, V.*

$$–$$$ 🏨 **Holiday Inn Beach Resort.** Nestled amid natural dunes
and oaks in a secluded oceanfront setting, this hotel has a
private beach, but its rooms with balconies still don't have
an ocean view. Bicycles are available for rent. ⊠ *200 S.
Beachview Dr., Jekyll Island 31527,* ☎ *912/635–3311 or
800/753–5955. 206 rooms. Restaurant, lobby lounge,
pool, 2 tennis courts, playground. AE, D, DC, MC, V.*

RENTALS

Jekyll's more than 200 **rental cottages and condos** are han-
dled by **Jekyll Realty** (⊠ Box 13096, Jekyll Island 31527,
☎ 912/635–3301, ℻ 912/635–3303) and **Parker-Kaufman
Realty** (⊠ Box 13126, Jekyll Island 31527, ☎ 912/635–
2512, ℻ 912/635–2190).

Outdoor Activities and Sports

GOLF

Jekyll has 63 holes of golf including three 18-hole courses
with a main clubhouse (⊠ Capt. Wylly Rd., ☎ 912/635–
2368) and a nine-hole course known as the Historic Ocean-
side Nine (⊠ Beachview Dr., ☎ 912/635–2170), where
millionaires used to play.

TENNIS

The **Jekyll Island Tennis Center** (⊠ Capt. Wylly Rd., ☎ 912/
635–3154) has 13 clay courts, with seven lighted for night-
time play; it hosts eight U.S.T.A.-sanctioned tournaments
throughout the year.

WATER PARK

Summer Waves, an 11-acre water park, has an 18,000-square-ft wave pool, water slides, a children's activity pool with two slides, and a circular river for tubing and rafting, but outside equipment is not permitted. ⊠ *210 S. Riverview Dr.,* ☎ *912/635–2074.* ☞ *$12.50.* ⊙ *Memorial Day– Labor Day, plus selected weekends in May and Sept., Sun.– Fri. 10–6, Sat. 10–8.*

St. Simons Island

❸ *6 mi from Brunswick.*

As large as Manhattan, with more than 14,000 year-round residents, St. Simons is the Golden Isles' most complete resort destination. Fortunately, the accelerated development in recent years has failed to spoil the natural beauty of the island's regal live oaks, beaches, and salt marshes. Visits are highlighted by swimming and sunning, golf, biking, hiking, fishing, horseback riding, touring historic sites, and feasting on fresh local seafood at more than 50 restaurants.

The **Brunswick and the Golden Isles Visitors Center** (⊠ 2000 Glynn Ave., Brunswick 31520, ☎ 912/264–5337, 912/265–5338, or 800/933–2627) provides helpful information.

Many sights and activities are in the **village** area along Mallery Street at the more developed south end of the island, where there are shops, several restaurants, pubs, and a popular public pier. A quaint "trolley" takes visitors on a 1½-hour guided tour of the island, leaving from near the pier, several times a day in high season, less frequently in winter; cost is $10.

Neptune Park (⊠ 550 Beachview Dr., ☎ 912/638–2393), on the island's south end, has picnic tables, a children's play park, miniature golf, and beach access. A swimming pool, with showers and rest rooms, is open each summer in the **Neptune Park Casino.**

St. Simons Lighthouse, a beacon since 1872, is virtually the symbol of St. Simons. The **Museum of Coastal History** in the lightkeeper's cottage has a permanent exhibit of coastal history. ⊠ *101 12th St.,* ☎ *912/638–4666.* ☞ *$3, including lighthouse.* ⊙ *Mon.–Sat. 10–5, Sun. 1:30–5.*

At the burgeoning north end of the island there's a marina, a golf club, and a housing development, as well as **Fort Frederica National Monument,** the ruins of a fort built by English troops in the mid-1730s as a bulwark against a Spanish invasion from Florida. Around the fort are the foundations of homes and shops. Start at the **National Park Service Visitors Center,** which has a film and displays. ⊠ *Off Frederica Rd. just past Christ Episcopal Church,* ☏ *912/638–3639.* 🎟 *$4 per car.* ☉ *Daily 9–5.*

Consecrated in 1886 following an earlier structure's desecration by Union troops, the white-frame Gothic-style **Christ Episcopal Church** is surrounded by live oaks, dogwoods, and azaleas. The interior has beautiful stained-glass windows. ⊠ *Frederica Rd., St. Simons,* ☏ *912/638–8683.* 🎟 *Donations welcome.*

Dining and Lodging

$$ ✕ **Blanche's Courtyard.** In the village, this lively restaurant/nightclub is done in "Bayou Victorian" style, with lots of antiques and nostalgic memorabilia. The menu features seafood as well as basic steak and chicken. Blue crab soup is a local favorite, and the huge seafood platter could easily feed two. Be sure to taste the popular apple fritters. A ragtime band plays for dancers on Saturday. ⊠ *440 Kings Way,* ☏ *912/638–3030. AE, DC, MC, V. No lunch.*

$–$$ ✕ **Alfonza's Olde Plantation Supper Club.** Down-home versions of seafood, superb steaks, and plantation fried chicken are served in a gracious and relaxed environment. ⊠ *171 Harrington La.,* ☏ *912/638–9883. Reservations essential. D, DC, MC, V. Closed Sun. No lunch.*

$ ✕ **CJ's.** This tiny village-area restaurant serves the island's best Italian food. Deep-dish and thin-crust pizzas, pastas, and all of the menu's sandwiches draw a faithful local clientele. The limited seating capacity creates lengthy waits, but the cuisine is worth your patience, and take-out is available. ⊠ *405 Mallory St.,* ☏ *912/634–1022. Reservations not accepted. No credit cards. Lunch served late Mar.–late Sept.*

$ ✕ **Crab Trap.** One of the island's most popular spots, the Crab Trap offers a variety of fried, blackened, grilled, and broiled fresh seafood; oysters on the half shell; blue crab soup; heaps of batter fries; and hush puppies. The atmosphere is rustic-casual—every table has a hole in the middle for depositing corncobs and shrimp shells. ⊠ *1209 Ocean Blvd.,* ☎ *912/638–3552. Reservations not accepted. MC, V.*

$$$$ ⊡ **Sea Palms Golf and Tennis Resort.** A contemporary resort complex with fully furnished villas, most with kitchens, nestles on an 800-acre site. Bicycles are available for rent. ⊠ *5445 Frederica Rd., St. Simons Island 31522,* ☎ *912/ 638–3351 or 800/841–6268,* FAX *912/634–8029. 154 rooms. 2 pools, 27-hole golf course, tennis court, children's programs. AE, DC, MC, V.*

$$–$$$$ ⊡ **King and Prince Beach and Golf Resort.** This hotel faces the beach. Guest rooms are spacious, and villas offer two or three bedrooms. The villas are owned by private individuals, so the total number available for rent varies from time to time. ⊠ *Box 20798, 201 Arnold Rd., St. Simons Island 31522,* ☎ *912/638–3631 or 800/342–0212,* FAX *912/634–1720. 139 rooms, 42 villas. 2 restaurants, lounge, indoor pool, 4 outdoor pools, golf privileges, 4 tennis courts, bicycles. AE, D, MC, V.*

$$ ⊡ **Island Inn.** On wooded land just off one of the island's main streets, this newer antebellum-style motel offers convenience and privacy with its efficiency accommodations. Continental breakfast is included, and complimentary wine and cheese are served Monday through Thursday from 5:30 to 6:30 PM. ⊠ *Plantation Village, 301 Main St., St. Simons Island 31522,* ☎ *912/638–7805 or 800/673– 6323. 74 rooms. Pool, hot tub, convention center, meeting rooms. AE, D, MC, V.*

$$ ⊡ **Queen's Court.** This family-oriented complex in the village has clean, modest rooms with shower-baths, some with kitchenettes. The grounds, with their ancient live oaks, are beautiful. ⊠ *437 Kings Way, St. Simons Island 31522,* ☎ *912/638–8459. 23 rooms. Pool. MC, V.*

RENTALS

For St. Simons **condo and cottage rentals,** contact **Golden Isles Realty** (⊠ 330 Mallory St., St. Simons Island 31522, ☎ 912/638–8623 or 800/337–3106, FAX 912/638–8624) and **Trupp–Hodnett Enterprises** (⊠ 520 Ocean Blvd., St. Simons Island 31522, ☎ 912/638–5450 or 800/627– 6850).

Sea Island

★ ❹ *5 mi from St. Simons Island.*

Separated from St. Simons Island by a narrow waterway and a good many steps up the social ladder, Sea Island has been the domain of the well-heeled and the **Cloister Hotel** since 1928. The Cloister still lives up to its celebrity status. Guests lodge in spacious, comfortably appointed rooms and suites in the Spanish Mediterranean hotel, designed by Florida architect Addison Mizner. The owners of the 180 or so private cottages and villas treat the hotel like a country club, and their tenants may use the hotel's facilities. Contact **Sea Island Cottage Rentals** (⊠ Box 30351, Sea Island 31561, ☎ 912/638–5112 or 800/732–4752, FAX 912/638–5824).

For recreation, there are 54 holes of golf, tennis, swimming in pools or at the beach, skeet shooting, horseback riding, sailing, biking, lawn games, and surf and deep-sea fishing. After dinner, guests dance to live music in the lounge. All meals are included in the rate.

Like a person of some years, the Cloister has its eccentricities. Credit cards are not honored, but personal checks are accepted. Gentlemen must cover their arms in the dining rooms. A complete and superb spa facility opened in 1989 in a beautiful building of its own; it has a fully equipped workout room, daily aerobics classes, personal trainers, facials and massages, and other beauty treatments. There is no entrance gate, and nonguests are free to admire the beautifully planted grounds and to drive past the mansions lining Sea Island Drive. Space permitting, they may also play at the Sea Island Golf Course (on St. Simons) and dine in the main dining room.

⊠ *The Cloister, Sea Island 31561, ☎ 912/638–3611 or 800/732–4752 reservations, FAX 912/638–5823. 262 rooms. 4 restaurants, 2 pools, spa, health club, 54-hole golf course, 18 tennis courts, concierge, business services, airport shuttle. No credit cards. High season (Mar. 15–May): $324–$638 for 2, including 3 meals daily; low season (Dec.–Feb. 14—excluding holiday times): $248–$366.*

Little St. Simons Island

★ ❺ *10–15 mins by ferry from the Hampton River Club Marina on St. Simons Island.*

Six miles long, 2 to 3 mi wide, skirted by Atlantic beaches and salt marshes teeming with birds and wildlife, this privately owned resort is custom-made for Robinson Crusoe–style getaways. The island's only development is a rustic but comfortable guest compound. Rates include all meals. Guided tours, horseback rides, canoe trips, fly-fishing lessons, and other extras can be arranged, some for no additional charge. Inquire about children, as there are some limitations. In summer, day tours may be arranged.

The island's forests and marshes are inhabited by deer, armadillos, horses, raccoons, 'gators, otters, and more than 200 species of birds. Guests are free to walk the 6 mi of undisturbed beaches, swim in the mild surf, fish from the dock, and seine for shrimp and crabs in the marshes. There are also horses to ride, nature walks with experts, and other island explorations via boat or the back of a pickup truck. From June through September, up to 10 nonguests per day may visit the island by reservation; the $70 cost includes the ferry to the island, an island tour by truck, lunch at the lodge, and a beach walk.

Dining and Lodging

$$$$ ✕🏠 **River Lodge and Cedar House.** Up to 24 guests can be accommodated in the lodge and house. Each has four bedrooms with twin or king-size beds, private decks, and private baths. In cool weather, a huge fireplace in each lodge's central living room dispels any chill. A large screened porch across the back permits beautiful views of the glorious sunsets. Two other lodges have two bedrooms each; one with private and the other with shared bath. None of the rooms is air-conditioned, but ceiling fans make sleeping comfortable. The rates include all meals and dinner wines (complimentary cocktails available). Meals often include fresh fish, pecan pie, and home-baked breads. The properties also provide transportation from St. Simons Island, transportation on the island, and interpretive guides. ✉ *21078 Little St. Simons Island 31522,* ☎ *912/638–7472,* ℻ *912/634–1811. 8 rooms. Pool, horseback riding, fishing. MC, V.*

Okefenokee National Wildlife Refuge

40 mi from Brunswick, 38 mi from St. Marys.

6 Covering 730 square mi of southeast Georgia and spilling over into northeast Florida, **The Okefenokee,** with its mysterious rivers and lakes, bristles with seen and unseen life. Scientists agree that the Okefenokee, the largest intact freshwater wetlands in the contiguous United States, is not duplicated anywhere else on earth. The impenetrable Pinhook Swamp to the south, part of the same ecosystem, adds another 100 square mi. If the term swamp denotes a dark, dank place, the Okefenokee is never that. Instead, it is actually a vast peat bog with numerous and varied landscapes, including aquatic prairies, towering virgin cypress, sandy pine islands, and lush subtropical hammocks. During the last Ice Age 10,000 years ago, it was part of the ocean flow. Peat began building up 7,000 years ago atop of a mound of clay, now 120 ft above sea level. Two rivers, the St. Marys and the Suwanee, flow out of it. It provides at least a part-time habitat for myriad species of birds, mammals, reptiles, amphibians, and fish.

As you travel by canoe or speedboat among the water lilies and the great stands of live oaks and cypress, be on the lookout for, among many others, alligators, otters, bobcats, raccoons, opossums, white-tailed deer, turtles, bald eagles, red-tailed hawks, egrets, muskrats, herons, cranes, and red-cockaded woodpeckers. The black bears tend to be more reclusive.

Seminole Indians, in their migrations south toward Florida's Everglades, once took refuge in the Okefenokee. The last Native Americans to occupy the area, they were evicted by the Army and Georgia's militia in the 1830s. When the Okefenokee acquired its present status of federal preserve (1937), the white homesteaders on its fringe were forced out.

Noting the many floating islands, the Seminole named this unique combination of land and water "Land of the Quivering Earth." If you have the rare fortune to walk one of these bogs, you will find the earth does indeed quiver, rather like fruit gelatin in a bowl.

Entrances to the swamp are at its northern, eastern, and western edges, and though all enable you to tour the swamp by boat or boardwalk, each provides slightly different experiences. The eastern entrance, near Folkston, at U.S. Fish & Wildlife Service Headquarters in the Suwanee Canal Recreation Area (☞ *below*) offers the most quiet, undisturbed view of the swamp. For a quick look your best bet is the north entrance, near Waycross, which has the Okefenokee Swamp Park (☞ *below*), a private nonprofit development. The western entrance, outside Fargo, accesses the 80-acre Stephen C. Foster State Park (☞ *below*), one of the few state parks within a national wildlife refuge. You may take an overnight canoe/camping trip into the interior, but the Okefenokee is a wildlife refuge and designated national wilderness, not a park. Access is restricted by permit. The best way to see the Okefenokee up close is to take a day trip at one of the three gateways. Plan your visit between April and September to avoid the biting insects that emerge in May, especially in the dense interior.

South of Waycross, via U.S. 1, **Okefenokee Swamp Park** has orientation programs, exhibits, observation areas, wilderness walkways, an outdoor museum of pioneer life, and boat tours into the swamp that reveal its ecological uniqueness. A boardwalk and 90-ft tower are excellent places to glimpse cruising 'gators and a variety of birds. You may arrange for guided boat tours at an additional cost. ⊠ *5700 Swamp Park Rd., Waycross 31501,* ☎ *912/283–0583,* FAX *912/283–0023.* 🖃 *$8, additional costs for tour packages.* ☉ *Summer, daily 9–6:30; spring, fall, and winter, 9–5:30.*

Stephen C. Foster State Park, 18 mi from Fargo via Route 177, is an 80-acre island park entirely within the Okefenokee National Wildlife Refuge. The park encompasses a large cypress and black gum forest, a majestic backdrop for one of the thickest growths of vegetation in the southeastern United States. Park naturalists leading boat tours will spill out a wealth of Okefenokee lore while you observe alligators, birds, and native trees and plants. You may also take a self-guided excursion in rental canoes and a motorized, flat-bottomed boat. Camping and cabins also are available here (☞ Camping, *below*). ⊠ *Fargo 31631,* ☎ *912/637–5274.* 🖃 *$5 per vehicle to National Wildlife*

Refuge. ⊗ *Mar.–Sept. 15, daily 6:30 AM–8:30 PM; Sept. 16–Feb., daily 7–7.*

Suwanee Canal Recreation Area, 8 mi south of Folkston via GA 121/23, is administered by the U.S. Fish and Wildlife Service. Stop first at the Visitor Information Center, with exhibits on the Okefenokee's flora and fauna. A boardwalk takes you over the water to a 50-ft observation tower. The concession has equipment rentals and daily food service; you may sign up here for one- or two-hour guided boat tours. Hikers, bicyclists, and private motor vehicles are welcome on the Swamp Island Drive; several interpretive walking trails may be taken along the way. Picnicking is allowed. Wilderness canoeing and camping in the Okefenokee's interior is by reserved fee permit only. Permits are hard to get especially in cool weather. Call refuge headquarters (☎ 912/496–3331) when it opens at 7 AM EXACTLY two months in advance of the desired starting date. Guided overnight canoe trips can be arranged by refuge concessionaire Carl E. Glenn Jr. ⊠ *Rte. 2, Box 3325, Folkston 31537,* ☎ *912/496–7156 or 800/792–6796. Refuge headquarters:* ⊠ *Rte. 2, Box 3330, Folkston, 31537,* ☎ *912/496–7836.* 🖃 *Park is free; $4 per car; 1-hr tours $8; 2-hr tours $16.* ⊗ *Refuge Mar.–Sept. 10, daily 7 AM–7:30 PM; Sept. 11–Feb., daily 8–6.*

Camping

$–$$ 🏕 **Stephen C. Foster State Park.** The park has furnished two-room cottages and campsites with water, electricity, rest rooms, and showers. Because of roaming wildlife and poachers, and because the park is inside the refuge, the gates close between sunset and sunrise. If you're staying overnight, stop for groceries before you get there. ⊠ *Fargo 31631,* ☎ *912/637–5274 or 800/864–7275.*

$ 🏕 **Laura S. Walker State Park.** Named for a Waycross teacher who championed conservation, the park, 9 mi from Okefenokee Swamp Park, offers campsites for $12, with electrical and water hookups. Be sure to pick up food and supplies on the way to the park. Boating and skiing are permitted on the 100-acre lake, and there's an 18-hole championship golf course, with all amenities. Cost is $17; carts $16. ⊠ *5653 Laura Walker Rd., Waycross 31503,* ☎ *912/287–4900. Picnic areas, pool, fishing, playground.*

The Golden Isles and the Okefenokee A to Z

Arriving, Departing, and Getting Around

BY CAR

From Brunswick by car, take the Jekyll Island Causeway for $2 per car to Jekyll Island, and the Torras Causeway to St. Simons and Sea Island. You can get by without a car on Jekyll Island and Sea Island, but you'll need one on St. Simons. You cannot bring a car to Cumberland Island or Little St. Simons.

To get to Okefenokee from Savannah, take I-95 South to Kingsland/St. Mary's (exit 2). Head West on Highway 40/ Okefenokee Parkway (to the right). Follow signs to Folkston and then signs for the refuge. Take a right, then left in front of courhouse and go straight across U.S. 1.

BY FERRY

Cumberland Island and Little St. Simons are accessible only by ferry or private launch (☞ *above*).

BY PLANE

The Golden Isles are served by **Glynco Jetport,** 6 mi north of Brunswick, which is served in turn by Delta affiliate **Atlantic Southeast Airlines** (☎ 800/282–3424) with flights from Atlanta.

Visitor Information

Georgia has centralized park reservations (Reservation Resource) for the state's **Department of Natural Resources** parks. For reservations, call 800/864–7275. In metropolitan Atlanta, the reservation number is 770/398–7275. For general park information, call 404/656–3530.

4 Charleston

AT FIRST GLIMPSE, Charleston resembles an 18th-century etching come to life, linking past with present. Its low-profile skyline is punctuated with the spires and steeples of 181 churches, representing 25 denominations—the reason that Charleston, known for religious freedom during its formation, is called the "Holy City." Parts of the city appear frozen in time; block after block of old downtown structures have been preserved and restored for residential and commercial use, and some brick and cobblestone streets remain. Many of its treasured double-galleried antebellum homes are now authentically furnished house museums. Charleston has survived three centuries of epidemics, earthquakes, fires, and hurricanes, and it is today one of the South's loveliest and best-preserved cities. It is not a museum, however: Throughout the year festivals (☞ Festivals *in* Nightlife and the Arts, *below*) add excitement and sophistication. Culturally vibrant, the city nurtures theater, dance, music, and visual arts, showcased each spring during the internationally acclaimed Spoleto Festival USA.

Updated by Mary Sue Lawrence

Besides the historic district, a visit to the city can easily include nearby towns, plantations and outstanding gardens, and historic sites, whether you're exploring Mount Pleasant or the area west of the Ashley River.

EXPLORING CHARLESTON

The Historic District

In a fairly compact area you'll find churches, museums, and lovely views at every turn. Along the Battery, on the point of a narrow peninsula bounded by the Ashley and Cooper rivers, handsome mansions in the "Charleston style," surrounded by gardens, face the harbor. Their distinctive look is reminiscent of the West Indies. Before coming to the Carolinas in the late 17th century, many early British colonists had first settled on Barbados and other Caribbean islands, where they'd built houses with high ceilings and broad piazzas at each level, to catch the sea breezes. In

Charleston, they adapted these designs. One new type—narrow two- to four-story "single houses" built at right angles to the street—emerged partly because buildings were taxed according to frontage length.

Numbers in the text correspond to numbers in the margin and on the Charleston map.

A Good Walk

Before you begin touring, drop by the **Visitor Information Center** ① for an overview of the city and tickets for shuttle services if you want to give your feet a break. Start at the **Charleston Museum** ② across the street, with its large decorative arts collection; then go right on Meeting Street, turning right on Ann Street and walking to Elizabeth Street to the palatial **Aiken–Rhett House** ③. After touring the house, head down Elizabeth Street and turn right on John Street for the **Joseph Manigault Mansion** ④, another impressive house museum dating to the early 1800s. From here, return to Meeting Street, walking south toward Calhoun Street, passing the **Old Citadel Building** ⑤, recently converted into the Embassy Suites. Take a left on Calhoun Street; a half block down is the **Emanuel African Methodist Episcopal Church** ⑥, where Denmark Vesey was a member. From here, you may want to use the shuttle bus DASH to give your feet a rest, or cross the street to Marion Square Mall for a drink and a break.

Retrace your steps on Calhoun Street (passing the Francis Marion Hotel, in the 1920s the highest building in the Carolinas) continuing two blocks west to St. Phillips Street, where you left to end up in the midst of the romantic campus of the **College of Charleston** ⑦, the oldest municipal college in the country. Enter through one of the gated openings on St. Phillips Street for a stroll under the many moss-draped trees. Then head east to King Street, Charleston's main shopping thoroughfare, and turn right; turn left on Hasell Street to see **Congregation Beth Elohim** ⑧, a Greek Revival building. Keep walking down Hasell Street, turning right on Meeting Street and then left down Pinckney Street to the **American Military Museum** ⑨. Two blocks to the south are **Market Hall** ⑩ and the bustling **Old City Market** ⑪. Now is a good time for a carriage tour, many of which leave from here (☞ Contacts and Resources *in* Charleston A to Z, *below*).

Aiken-Rhett
House, **3**

American
Military
Museum, **9**

Calhoun
Mansion, **26**

Charleston
Museum, **2**

Charleston Pl., **12**

Circular
Cong. Church, **16**

City Hall, **22**

College of
Charleston, **7**

Congregation
Beth Elohim, **8**

Dock Street
Theatre, **20**

Edmondston-
Alston House, **27**

Emanuel AME
Church, **6**

French Protestant
(Huguenot)
Church, **19**

Gibbes Museum
of Art, **15**

Heyward-
Washington
House, **24**

Joseph Manigault
Mansion, **4**

Market Hall, **10**

Nathaniel Russell
House, **25**

Old Citadel
Building/
Embassy Suites, **5**

Old City
Market, **11**

Old Exchange
Building/Provost
Dungeon, **21**

Old Powder
Magazine, **17**

St. John's, **13**

St. Michael's, **23**

St. Philip's, **18**

Unitarian
Church, **14**

Visitor
Information
Center, **1**

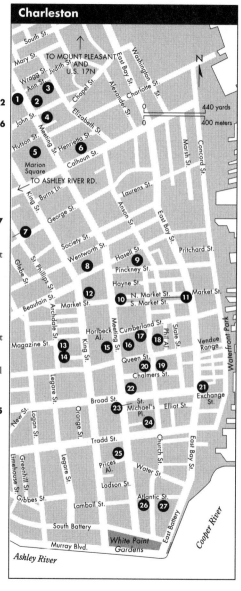

Across Meeting Street is the classy **Charleston Place** ⑫, with its graceful hotel and cluster of shops. You can browse from one end to the other, exiting on King Street.

Facing you on the opposite corner is the new Saks Fifth Avenue; cross the street and walk a block down Market Street, turning left on quiet Archdale Street to wander through the **St. John's Lutheran Church** ⑬ and the peaceful graveyard of the **Unitarian Church** ⑭. Turn left on Queen Street at the bottom of Archdale and walk two blocks to Meeting Street, where you turn left for the **Gibbes Museum of Art** ⑮, with its spectacular stained-glass dome. Across the street is the **Circular Congregational Church** ⑯. Behind it, on cobblestone Cumberland Street, is the **Old Powder Magazine** ⑰. To the left as you face the building, you'll catch a glimpse of the steeple of **St. Philip's Episcopal Church** ⑱, famous in the city's skyline; it's around the corner on Church Street.

Cross over to picturesque Church Street to the **French Huguenot Church** ⑲ and the **Dock Street Theatre** ⑳ across the street. You might detour here down Queen Street and along Vendue Range to Waterfront Park, to relax in a bench swing overlooking beautiful river views, dramatic fountains, and a fishing pier. Or you can walk south along the park's landscaped garden path to Exchange Street, turning down it to Broad Street and the **Old Exchange Building/Provost Dungeon** ㉑, used to hold prisoners during the American Revolution. Two blocks down Broad Street are the Four Corners of Law, including **City Hall** ㉒, with some historical displays and portraits, and **St. Michael's Episcopal Church** ㉓, the city's oldest surviving church. In the famously affluent neighborhood known as South of Broad are several of the city's lavish house museums: the **Heyward–Washington House** ㉔, a block south of Broad on Church Street; the **Nathaniel Russell House** ㉕ and the **Calhoun Mansion** ㉖, both on Meeting Street; and the **Edmondston–Alston House** ㉗ near the Battery. A park bench in the shade of White Point Gardens, overlooking the Battery, is a splendid, Charleston-style finish.

TIMING

Plan to spend at least a full day doing the bare bones of this walk. Most of the house museum tours last about 40 minutes, so you might choose two or three that interest you most, or split the walk in half, taking two days to enjoy it fully. If it's high summer, you'll likely be moving with the speed of a Southern drawl, so pace yourself and make use of all those Charleston benches.

Sights to See

❸ Aiken–Rhett House. This stately 1819 mansion, with original wallpaper, paint colors, and some furnishings, was the headquarters of Confederate general P. G. T. Beauregard during his 1864 Civil War defense of Charleston. The house, kitchen, slave quarters, and work yard are maintained much as they were when the original occupants lived here, making this one of the most complete examples of African-American urban life of the period. ⊠ *48 Elizabeth St.,* ☎ *803/723–1159.* ☞ *$6; combination ticket with Nathaniel Russell House (☞ below) $10.* ☉ *Mon.–Sat. 10–5, Sun. 1–5.*

✋ ❾ American Military Museum. The museum displays hundreds of uniforms and artifacts from all branches of service, dating from the Revolutionary War. Its collections also include antique toy soldiers, war toys, and miniatures and weaponry. ⊠ *40 Pinckney St.,* ☎ *803/723–9620.* ☞ *$5.* ☉ *Mon.–Sat. 10–6, Sun. 1–6.*

㉖ Calhoun Mansion. Opulent by Charleston standards, this is an interesting example of Victorian taste. Built in 1876, it's notable for ornate plasterwork, fine wood moldings, and a 75-ft domed ceiling. ⊠ *16 Meeting St.,* ☎ *803/722–8205.* ☞ *$10.* ☉ *Feb.–Dec., Wed.–Sun. 10–4.*

★ ✋ ❷ Charleston Museum. Housed in a $6 million contemporary complex, this is the oldest city museum in the United States. Founded in 1773, it is especially strong in South Carolina decorative arts. The 500,000 items in the collection—in addition to Charleston silver, fashions, toys, snuff boxes, and the like—include objects relating to natural history, archaeology, and ornithology. The Discover Me Room, designed just for children, has computers and other hands-on exhibits. Two historic homes—the ☞ **Joseph Manigault Mansion** and the ☞ **Heyward–Washington House**—are part of the museum. ⊠ *360 Meeting St.,* ☎ *803/722–2996.* ☞ *$6; combination ticket for museum and houses $15; for 2 sites $10.* ☉ *Mon.–Sat. 9–5, Sun. 1–5.*

⑫ Charleston Place. The city's only world-class hotel, this Orient Express property is flanked by a four-story complex of upscale boutiques and specialty shops (☞ Shopping, *below*). You might peek into the lobby or have cocktails or tea in the intimate Lobby Lounge. The garage and reception area are entered on Hasell Street between Meeting and King streets. ⊠ *130 Market St.,* ☎ *803/722–4900.*

⑯ Circular Congregational Church. The corners of this unusual Romanesque church were rounded off, they say, so the devil would have no place to hide. Simple but pretty, it has a beamed, vaulted ceiling. ⊠ *150 Meeting St.,* ☎ *803/577–6400.* ☺ *Call for tour schedule.*

㉒ City Hall. The intersection of Meeting and Broad streets is known as the Four Corners of Law, representing the laws of nation, state, city, and church. On the northeast corner is graceful City Hall, dating from 1801. The second-floor Council Chamber has interesting historical displays and portraits, including John Trumbull's 1791 satirical portrait of George Washington and Samuel F. B. Morse's likeness of James Monroe. ⊠ *80 Broad St.,* ☎ *803/577–6970 or 803/724–3799.* ☖ *Free.* ☺ *Weekdays 10–5.*

❼ College of Charleston. The lovely, tree-shaded campus of this college, founded in 1770, has a graceful main building, the Randolph House (1828), designed by Philadelphia architect William Strickland. It forms a romantic backdrop for the Cistern, a grassy "stage" where concerts and many activities take place. Within the college, centered at the corner of George and St. Phillips streets, is the **Avery Research Center for African-American History and Culture,** which traces the heritage of Lowcountry African-Americans. ⊠ *Avery Research Center, 125 Bull St.,* ☎ *803/727–2009.* ☖ *Free.* ☺ *Mon.–Sat. noon–5; mornings by appointment.*

❽ Congregation Beth Elohim. Considered one of the nation's finest examples of Greek Revival architecture, this temple was built in 1840 to replace an earlier one—the birthplace of American Reform Judaism in 1824—that was destroyed by fire. ⊠ *90 Hasell St.,* ☎ *803/723–1090.* ☺ *Weekdays 10–noon.*

NEED A
BREAK?

On your way to the cluster of sights around Meeting Street, pick up a batch of Charleston's famed benne wafers at **Olde Colony Bakery** (⊠ 280 King St., between Society and Wentworth, ☎ 803/722-2147). *Benne* is an African word that slaves used to describe the sesame seeds on these delicacies.

⑳ Dock Street Theatre. Built on the site of one of the nation's first playhouses, the building combines the reconstructed early Georgian playhouse and the preserved Old Planter's Hotel (circa 1809). The theater, which offers fascinating backstage views, welcomes tours except when technical work for a show is under way. ⊠ *135 Church St.,* ☎ *803/720–3968.* ⌸ *Free tours; call ahead for ticket prices and performance times.* ☉ *Weekdays 10–4.*

㉗ Edmondston–Alston House. With commanding views of Charleston Harbor, this imposing home was built in 1825 in the late Federal style and transformed into a Greek Revival structure during the 1840s. It is tastefully furnished with antiques, portraits, Piranesi prints, silver, and fine china. ⊠ *21 E. Battery,* ☎ *803/722-7171.* ⌸ *$7.* ☉ *Tues.–Sat. 10–4:30, Sun.–Mon. 1:30–4:30.*

➏ Emanuel African Methodist Episcopal Church. Home of the South's oldest AME congregation, the church had its beginnings in 1818. It was closed in 1822 when authorities learned that Denmark Vesey had used the sanctuary to plan his slave insurrection, but the church reopened in 1865 at the present site. ⊠ *110 Calhoun St.,* ☎ *803/722-2561.* ☉ *Daily 9–4; call ahead for tour.*

⑲ French Protestant (Huguenot) Church. This church is the only one in the country still using the original Huguenot liturgy, which can be heard in a special service held each spring. ⊠ *110 Church St.,* ☎ *803/722-4385.* ⌸ *Donations welcome.* ☉ *Weekdays 10–12:30 and 2–4.*

NEED A
BREAK?

For a great view of the harbor, the **Vendue Inn** (☞ Lodging, *below*) on Vendue Range, at the end of Queen Street, offers lunch, drinks, and appetizers alfresco on its one-of-a-kind Rooftop Lounge.

⑮ Gibbes Museum of Art. The collections of American art include notable 18th- and 19th-century portraits of Carolinians and an outstanding group of more than 400 miniature portraits. Don't miss the miniature rooms—intricately detailed with fabrics and furnishings and nicely displayed in shadow boxes inset in dark-paneled walls—or the Tiffany-style stained-glass dome in the rotunda. ⊠ *135 Meeting St.,* ☎ *803/722–2706.* ✑ *$5.* ☉ *Tues.–Sat. 10–5, Sun.–Mon. 1–5.*

㉔ Heyward–Washington House. Built in 1772 by rice king Daniel Heyward, this home was the backdrop for Dubose Heyward's book *Porgy,* also beloved as the folk opera *Porgy and Bess.* The neighborhood, known as Cabbage Row, is central to Charleston's African-American history. President George Washington stayed in the house during his 1791 visit. It is full of fine period furnishings by such local craftsmen as Thomas Elfe, and its restored 18th-century kitchen is the only one in Charleston open to visitors. ⊠ *87 Church St.,* ☎ *803/722–0354.* ✑ *$6; for combination ticket, ☞ Charleston Museum, above.* ☉ *Mon.–Sat. 10–5, Sun. 1–5.*

④ Joseph Manigault Mansion. A National Historic Landmark and an outstanding example of neoclassical architecture, this home was designed by Charleston architect Gabriel Manigault in 1803 and is noted for its carved-wood mantels and elaborate plasterwork. Furnishings are British and French but primarily Charleston antiques, and include rare tricolor Wedgwood pieces. ⊠ *350 Meeting St.,* ☎ *803/723–2926.* ✑ *$6; for combination ticket, ☞ Charleston Museum, above.* ☉ *Mon.–Sat. 10–5, Sun. 1–5.*

⑩ Market Hall. Built in 1841 and modeled after the Temple of Nike in Athens, this imposing landmark building includes the **Confederate Museum,** where the Daughters of the Confederacy preserve and display flags, uniforms, swords, and other Civil War memorabilia. The museum, heavily damaged by Hurricane Hugo in 1989, is closed for renovation and may remain so through 1999; however, costumed guides sometimes stand outside and describe the facility for visitors. The collection is temporarily housed at 34 Pitt Street; admission is $2, and it's open Saturday noon–4, Sunday 1–4. ⊠ *88 Meeting St.,* ☎ *803/723–1541.*

★ **㉕ Nathaniel Russell House.** One of the nation's finest examples of Adams-style architecture, the Nathaniel Russell

House was built in 1808. The interior is notable for its ornate detailing, its lavish period furnishings, and a "flying" circular staircase that spirals three stories with no apparent support. ⊠ *51 Meeting St.,* ☎ *803/724–8481.* ☜ *$6; combination ticket with Aiken–Rhett House (☞ above) $10.* ☼ *Mon.–Sat. 10–5, Sun. 2–5.*

❺ Old Citadel Building/Embassy Suites. Built in 1822 to house state troops and arms, the Old Citadel Building faces Marion Square. This is where the Carolina Military College—The Citadel—had its start. The fortresslike building is now the Embassy Suites Historic Charleston (☞ Lodging, *below*), and The Citadel is now on the Ashley River.

☾ ⓫ Old City Market. A series of low sheds that once housed produce and fish markets, this area is often called the Slave Market, although Charlestonians dispute that slaves ever were sold there. It now has restaurants, shops, and "gimcracks and gee-gaws" for children, along with vegetable and fruit vendors and local "basket ladies" busy weaving and selling distinctive sweetgrass, pine-straw, and palmetto-leaf baskets—a craft passed through generations from their West African ancestors. ⊠ *Market St. between Meeting and E. Bay Sts.* ☼ *Daily 9 AM–sunset; hrs may vary.*

NEED A
BREAK?

Indulge the urge to munch on oysters on the half shell, steamed mussels, and clams at **A. W. Shucks** (☎ 803/723–1151) in State Street Market, across from the Market Square Food Court.

☾ ㉑ Old Exchange Building/Provost Dungeon. Originally a customs house, the British used it for prisoners during the Revolutionary War. Today a tableau of lifelike mannequins recalls this era. ⊠ *122 E. Bay St.,* ☎ *803/792–5020.* ☜ *$4.* ☼ *Daily 9–5.*

⓱ Old Powder Magazine. On one of Charleston's few remaining cobblestone thoroughfares, this structure was built in 1713 and used during the Revolutionary War. It is now a museum with costumes, furniture, armor, and other artifacts from 18th-century Charleston. Because the Historic Charleston Foundation is restoring the building, visitors can see the exterior only. Call ahead to see if tours have resumed. ⊠ *79 Cumberland St.,* ☎ *803/723–1623.*

⑬ St. John's Lutheran Church. This Greek Revival church was built in 1817 for a congregation that celebrated its 250th anniversary in 1992. Notice the fine craftsmanship in the delicate wrought-iron gates and fence. Musicians may be interested in the 1823 Thomas Hall organ case. ⊠ *5 Clifford St.,* ☎ *803/723–2426.* ⊙ *Weekdays 9:30–3.*

㉓ St. Michael's Episcopal Church. Modeled after London's St. Martin-in-the-Fields and completed in 1761, this is Charleston's oldest surviving church. Its steeple clock and bells were imported from England in 1764. ⊠ *14 St. Michael's Alley,* ☎ *803/723–0603.* ⊙ *Weekdays 9–5, Sat. 9–noon.*

⑱ St. Philip's Episcopal Church. The graceful late-Georgian church is the second on its site, built in 1838 and restored in 1994. In the graveyard on the church's side of the street, Charlestonians are buried; in the graveyard on the other side, "foreigners" lie (including John C. Calhoun, who was from Abbeville, South Carolina). ⊠ *146 Church St.,* ☎ *803/722–7734.* ⊙ *By appointment.*

⑭ Unitarian Church. Completed in 1787, this church was re-modeled in the mid-19th century after plans inspired by the Chapel of Henry VII in Westminster Abbey. The Gothic fan-tracery ceiling was added during that renovation. There's an entrance to the church grounds on 161½–163 King Street, amid the antiques shops there. The secluded and ro-mantically overgrown graveyard invites contemplation. ⊠ *8 Archdale St.,* ☎ *803/723–4617 weekdays 8:30–2:30.* ⊙ *Call ahead for visiting hrs.*

❶ Visitor Information Center. The center gives an introduction to the city and sells tickets for shuttle services (☞ *Getting Around in Charleston A to Z, below*). Parking is $1 per hour; the first hour is free if you purchase a shuttle pass. Take time to see *Forever Charleston,* an insightful 20-minute film. ⊠ *375 Meeting St.,* ☎ *803/853–8000 or 800/868–8118.* ▣ *$2.50 for film.* ⊙ *Mar.–Oct., daily 8:30–5:30; Nov.–Feb., daily 8:30–5; shows daily 9–5 on the ½ hr.*

Mount Pleasant and Vicinity

Across the Cooper River bridges, via U.S. 17N, is the town of Mount Pleasant, named not for a mountain or a hill, but for a plantation in England from which some of the area's settlers hailed. In its Old Village neighborhood are antebellum homes and a sleepy, old-time town center with shops and cafés. Along Shem Creek, where the local fishing fleet brings in the daily catch, are good seafood restaurants. Other attractions in the area include museums and plantations.

A Good Tour

There's enough adventure here to stretch over two days, especially if you're a war history buff. On the first day you might drive to **Patriots Point,** veering right off the Cooper River Bridge onto Coleman Boulevard in the direction of Sullivan's Island and the Isle of Palms. Turn right at the signs, then board the museum ships for tours. From here you can catch the ferry for a harbor ride to **Fort Sumter National Monument.** Later, continue along Coleman Boulevard and, just after crossing the boat-lined docks and restaurants at Shem Creek, turn right at Whilden Street for a drive through the Old Village. Returning to Coleman Boulevard, you'll pass The Common, a cluster of shops on your left. Stop here for the **Museum on the Common,** featuring a "Hurricane Hugo Revisited" exhibit: As you make your way across the Ben Sawyer Bridge to Sullivan's Island and the Isle of Palms, you'll see how the area has recovered from Hugo. Follow the signs to **Fort Moultrie.** Spend the rest of the day on the beach or bicycling through Sullivan's Island, a residential community scattered with turn-of-the-century beach houses, or the Isle of Palms, which has a pavilion and more abundant parking.

Another day, you can drive out U.S. 17 North 8 mi to **Boone Hall Plantation** and its famous Avenue of Oaks. Bring a picnic and rent bikes at **Palmetto Islands County Park,** across Boone Hall Creek from the plantation; you'll need a swimsuit for "Splash Island," a mini–water park.

TIMING

You need two days to see all the attractions here; if you have one day or less, choose a few based on your interests.

Sights to See

★ **Boone Hall Plantation.** You approach the plantation along one of the South's most majestic avenues of oaks, which were the model for the grounds of Tara in *Gone With the Wind*. The primary attraction is the grounds, with formal azalea and camellia gardens, as well as the original slave quarters—the only "slave street" still intact in the Southeast—and the cotton-gin house used in the made-for-television movies *North and South* and *Queen.* You may also tour the first floor of the classic columned mansion, which was built in 1935 incorporating woodwork and flooring from the original house. ⊠ *1235 Long Point Rd., off U.S. 17N,* ☎ *803/884–4371.* 🎫 *$10.* ☉ *Apr.–Labor Day, Mon.–Sat. 8:30–6:30, Sun. 1–5; Labor Day–Mar., Mon.–Sat. 9–5, Sun. 1–4.*

NEED A BREAK?

Driving north of Mount Pleasant along U.S. 17, you can stop and see **"basket ladies"** at roadside stands. If you have the heart to bargain, you *may* be able to purchase the baskets at somewhat lower prices than in Charleston. But remember that you are buying a nearly lost art, and sweetgrass is no longer plentiful in the wild.

☺ **Fort Moultrie.** Here Colonel William Moultrie's South Carolinians repelled a British assault in one of the first Patriot victories of the Revolutionary War. Completed in 1809, this is the third fort on this site at **Sullivan's Island,** which you'll reach on SC 703 off U.S. 17N. The interior has been restored. A 20-minute film tells the history of the fort. ⊠ *W. Middle St., Sullivan's Island,* ☎ *803/883–3123.* 🎫 *Free.* ☉ *Daily 9–5.*

★ ☺ **Fort Sumter National Monument.** This site, which can be reached from either Charleston's Municipal Marina or Patriot's Point, is on a man-made island in Charleston Harbor. It was here that the first shot of the Civil War was fired on April 12, 1861, by Confederate forces. After a 34-hour bombardment, Union forces surrendered and Confederate troops occupied Sumter, which became a symbol of Southern resistance. The Confederacy held the fort, despite almost continual bombardment, for nearly four years, and when it was finally evacuated it was a heap of rubble. Today National Park Service rangers conduct free guided tours of the restored structure, which includes a free museum (☎ *803/883–3123*) with historical displays. ☎ *803/722–1691.* 🎫 *Ferry fare $10.50.* ☉ *Tours usually leave from*

Municipal Marina daily at 9:30, noon, and 2:30, but they vary by season. Tours leave from Patriots Point daily at 10:45 and 1:30; Apr.–Labor Day, additional tour at 4.

🐚 **Museum on The Common.** This small museum has a Hurricane Hugo exhibit prepared by the South Carolina State Museum; it shows the 1989 storm damage through video and photos. ⊠ *217 Lucas St., Shem Creek Village,* ☎ *803/ 849–9000.* 🖃 *Free.* 🕙 *Mon.–Sat. 10–4.*

🐚 **Palmetto Islands County Park.** A Big Toy playground, 2-acre pond, paved trails, an observation tower, marsh boardwalks, and a "water island" can be enjoyed in this park across Boone Hall Creek from Boone Hall Plantation. Bicycles and pedal boats can be rented in season. ⊠ *U.S. 17N, ½ mi past Snee Farm, turn left onto Long Point Rd.,* ☎ *803/884– 0832.* 🖃 *$1.* 🕙 *Apr., Sept., Oct., daily 9–6; May–Aug., daily 9–7; Nov.–Feb., daily 10–5; Mar., daily 10–6.*

★ 🐚 **Patriots Point.** Tours are offered on all vessels here at the world's largest naval and maritime museum, now home to the Medal of Honor Society. Berthed here are the aircraft carrier *Yorktown,* the World War II submarine *Clamagore,* the destroyer *Laffey,* the nuclear merchant ship *Savannah,* and the cutter *Ingham,* responsible for sinking a U-boat during World War II. The film *The Fighting Lady* is shown regularly aboard the *Yorktown,* and there is a Vietnam exhibit. ⊠ *Foot of Cooper River Bridges,* ☎ *803/884–2727.* 🖃 *$9.* 🕙 *Labor Day–Mar., daily 9–6:30; Apr.–Labor Day, daily 9–7:30.*

West of the Ashley River

The gardens and houses in this area are highlights of many visits to Charleston.

A Good Tour

Drayton Hall, Magnolia Plantations and Gardens, and Middletown Gardens are each a few miles apart along Ashley River Road, SC 61, about 10 mi northwest of downtown Charleston over the Ashley River Bridge. Still, you'll need time to see them all. One day you could spend a few hours exploring **Charles Towne Landing State Park,** veering off SC 61 onto Old Towne Road (SC 171); then finish your day at **Middleton Gardens.** Another day you might tour the majestic simplicity of **Drayton Hall** before continuing on to **Magnolia Plantations and Gardens** and all their splendor.

TIMING

Nature and garden enthusiasts can easily spend a full day at Magnolia Gardens, Middleton Gardens, or Charles Towne Landing State Park, so budget your time accordingly. Spring is a peak time for the gardens, although they are lovely throughout the year.

Sights to See

★ ☺ **Charles Towne Landing State Park.** Commemorating the site of the original 1670 Charleston settlement, this park on SC 171 North across the Ashley River Bridge has a reconstructed village and fortifications, English park gardens with bicycle trails and walkways, and a replica 17th-century vessel moored in the creek. In the animal park, species native to the region for three centuries roam freely—among them alligators, bison, pumas, bears, and wolves. Bicycle and kayak rentals and cassette and tram tours are available. ✉ *1500 Old Towne Rd.,* ☎ *803/852–4200.* ✑ *$5.* ⊘ *Memorial Day–Labor Day, daily 9–6; Labor Day–Memorial Day, daily 9–5.*

★ **Drayton Hall.** Considered the nation's finest example of unspoiled Georgian-Palladian architecture, this mansion is the only plantation house on the Ashley River to have survived the Civil War. A National Historic Landmark built between 1738 and 1742, it serves as an invaluable lesson in history as well as in architecture. Drayton Hall has been left unfurnished to highlight the original plaster moldings, opulent hand-carved woodwork, and other ornamental details. ✉ *3380 Ashley River Rd.,* ☎ *803/766–0188.* ✑ *$8.* ⊘ *Guided tours Mar.–Oct., daily 10–4; Nov.–Feb., daily 10–3.*

☺ **Magnolia Plantation and Gardens.** The 50-acre informal garden, begun in 1685, has a huge collection of azaleas and camellias. You can ride a tram for an overall tour with three stops. Nature lovers may canoe through the 125-acre Waterfowl Refuge, explore the 30-acre **Audubon Swamp Garden** along boardwalks and bridges, or walk or bicycle over 500 acres of wildlife trails. Tours of the manor house, built during Reconstruction, depict plantation life. You can also see the petting zoo and a miniature-horse ranch. ⊠ *Ashley River Rd.,* ☎ *803/571–1266 or 800/367–3517.* ☞ *$9; house tour $5 extra; tram tour $4 extra; swamp tour $10 alone or $4 extra; combination tour available.* ☼ *Daily 8–5:30.*

★ ☺ **Middleton Place.** The nation's oldest landscaped gardens, dating from 1741, are magnificently ablaze with camellias, magnolias, azaleas, roses, and flowers of all seasons planted in floral *allées* and terraced lawns, and around ornamental lakes. Much of the mansion was destroyed during the Civil War, but the south wing has been restored and houses impressive collections of silver, furniture, paintings, and historic documents. In the stable yard craftspeople use authentic tools and equipment to demonstrate spinning, blacksmithing, and other domestic skills from the plantation era. Farm animals, peacocks, and other creatures roam freely. The Middleton Place restaurant serves Lowcountry specialties for lunch daily; a gift shop carries local arts, crafts, and souvenirs. Also on the grounds is a modern, Danish-style inn (access to the gardens is included in the room price) with floor-to-ceiling windows dramatizing views of the Ashley River; here you can sign up for kayaking, canoeing, and biking tours. ⊠ *Ashley River Rd.,* ☎ *803/556–6020 or 800/ 782–3608.* ☞ *$14; house tours $7 extra.* ☼ *Daily 9–5; house tours Tues.–Sun. 10–4:30, Mon. 1:30–4:30.*

DINING

She-crab soup, sautéed shrimp, stuffed oysters, variations on pecan pie, and other Lowcountry specialties are served all over the Charleston area, but local chefs whip up some creative contemporary dishes as well. Known for outstanding eateries—ranging from fresh seafood houses to elegant French restaurants—Charleston is a mecca for gastronomes. Across the East Cooper Bridge, in trendy Mount Pleasant, there are a number of good restaurants. And don't write off grits until you've tasted them laced with cheese, topped with *tasso* (spiced ham) gravy, or folded into a veal or quail entrée.

CATEGORY	COST*
$$$$	over $40
$$$	$30–$40
$$	$20–$30
$	under $20

per person for a three-course meal, excluding drinks, service, and 5% tax

American

$$$ ✕ **Anson.** After an afternoon of strolling through the Old City Market, you can walk up Anson Street to one of the better restaurants in town. The softly lit, gilt-trimmed dining room is framed by about a dozen French windows; booths are anchored by marble-top tables. Anson's serves up dependable American fare—mainly seafood, chicken, and steak—with the occasional international twist in a whimsical special. Desserts are of the rich, Southern variety, so save room. ⊠ *12 Anson St.,* ☎ *803/577–0551. AE, D, DC, MC, V. No lunch.*

$$$ ✕ **Peninsula Grill.** Surrounded by olive green wall coverings, black iron chandeliers, and 18th-century-style portraits, diners at this new hot spot in the Planters Inn (☞ Lodging, *below*) can feast on such delights as lobster citron, wild mushroom grits with oysters, and New Zealand benne-seed-encrusted rack of lamb. For dessert, try the divine lemon tart with lemon sorbet, lemon crisps, and candied lemon. ⊠ *112 N. Market St.,* ☎ *803/723–0700. AE, D, DC, MC, V.*

$$ ✕ **Elliott's on the Square.** This elegant, streamlined restaurant in the newly renovated Francis Marion Hotel (☞ Lodging, *below*) has butter-color walls, black and gold accents, whimsical lighting, and a friendly, cozy bar. Here you can have breakfast or a varied lunch, from cheeseburgers and pasta to pulled duck and fried pot stickers. At dinner, seafood reigns: You might start with the fried oysters with red onion marmalade, or shrimp and basil beignets, and follow with grouper layered with phyllo pastry, spinach, and caramelized onions. ⊠ *387 King St.,* ☎ *803/724–8888. AE, D, DC, MC, V.*

$ ✕ **Mike Calder's Deli & Pub.** Soups, salads, sandwiches, daily home-cooked specials such as Creole seafood casseroles, and 15 different draft beers are offered in an "Old World" set-

Alice's Fine
Foods, **3**

Anson, **8**

Barbadoes
Room, **12**

Carolina's, **14**

Elliott's on the
Square, **4**

Gaulart and
Maliclet Cafe
Restaurant, **13**

Magnolias, **10**

Mike Calder's
Deli & Pub, **5**

Peninsula
Grill, **7**

Restaurant
Million, **11**

Slightly North of
Broad, **9**

Sticky Fingers, **6**

Supper at
Stacks, **2**

The Wreck, **1**

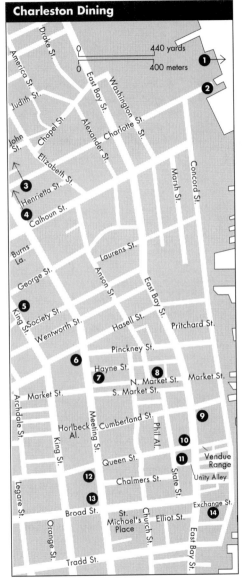

Charleston Dining

ting, once a pharmacy in the historic district. ⊠ *288 King St.,* ☎ *803/577–0123. No reservations. AE, D, MC, V. Closed Sun.*

French

$$$–
$$$$ ✕ **Restaurant Million.** This restaurant serves French nouvelle cuisine on Limoges china in a building dating to 1788. The rack of lamb and the five-course ($50) and three-course ($28) prix-fixe meals are outstanding. Downstairs at the casual and less expensive McCrady's (☎ 803/577–0025), inventive appetizers, soups, salads, and grills are served. ⊠ *2 Unity Alley,* ☎ *803/577–3141. Reservations essential in restaurant. Jacket and tie. AE, DC, MC, V. Closed Sun. No lunch in restaurant; no lunch Sat. in McCrady's.*

$–$$ ✕ **Gaulart and Maliclet Cafe Restaurant.** This casual, chic eatery serves Continental dishes—breads and pastries, soups, salads, sandwiches, and specials like seafood Normandy and chicken sesame. ⊠ *98 Broad St.,* ☎ *803/577–9797. AE, D, DC, MC, V. Closed Sun. No dinner Mon.*

Lowcountry

$$ ✕ **Carolina's.** Lively and bustling, Carolina's has long been a favorite. Black, white, and peach decor, terra-cotta tiles, and 1920s French posters create a casual bistro atmosphere. Fans return for the "appeteasers" and the late-night (until 1 AM) offerings, which include everything from smoked baby-back ribs to pasta with crawfish and tasso in cream sauce. Dinner entrées are selections from the grill: among them, pork tenderloin with Jamaican seasoning and salmon with cilantro, ginger, and lime butter. ⊠ *10 Exchange St.,* ☎ *803/724–3800. Reservations essential. D, MC, V. No lunch.*

$$ ✕ **Slightly North of Broad.** This high-ceiling haunt with brick
★ and stucco walls, and red wooden floors, has several seats looking directly into the exposed kitchen. From here you'll see chef Frank Lee laboring over his inventive—but hardly esoteric—dishes: sautéed quail filled with herbed chicken mousse; pad Thai noodles with shrimp, pork, and an authentic fish sauce; and corn-and-crab soup with spinach ravioli. You can order most items as either an appetizer or an entrée. The extensive wine list is moderately priced. A sis-

ter restaurant, Slightly Up the Creek (✉ 130 Mill St., ☎ 803/884–5005), at Shem Creek in Mount Pleasant, offers similarly fine food plus waterfront views. ✉ *192 E. Bay St.,* ☎ *803/723–3424. Reservations not accepted. AE, D, DC, MC, V. Closed Sun. No lunch Sat.*

Lowcountry/Southern

$$–$$$ ✕ **Magnolias.** This popular place, in an 1823 warehouse,
★ is cherished by Charlestonians and visitors alike. The magnolia theme is seen throughout in vivid Rod Goebel paintings, etched glass, wrought iron, and candlesticks. The "uptown/down South" cuisine shines in specialties like the "Down-South" egg roll stuffed with chicken and collard greens with spicy mustard sauce and sweet pepper puree. Equally innovative appetizers include seared yellow grits cakes with tasso gravy and yellow corn relish, and sautéed greens. There's even fried chicken with mashed potatoes and mushroom gravy and, for dessert, a heaping strawberry shortcake biscuit. You may also want to try the **Blossom Cafe** (✉ 171 E. Bay St., ☎ 803/722–9200), owned by the same people. ✉ *185 E. Bay St.,* ☎ *803/577–7771. Reservations essential. AE, DC, MC, V.*

$$ ✕ **Supper at Stacks.** Above the Guilds Inn, formal, prix-fixe, four-course Continental meals ($29) are presented in a grand dining room—the menu changes daily and depends largely on what's fresh. ✉ *101 Pitt St., Mount Pleasant,* ☎ *803/884–7009. Reservations essential for dinner. Jacket and tie. AE, MC, V. Closed Sun.–Mon. No lunch.*

$ ✕ **Alice's Fine Foods.** The food Southerners crave is here
★ in its original, beloved form: Baked or fried chicken, ribs, fried fish, or other entrées come with a choice of three vegetables, including green beans, collard greens, red rice, macaroni-and-cheese pie, okra and tomatoes, lima beans, rice and gravy, yams, and squash. ✉ *468–470 King St.,* ☎ *803/853–9366. MC, V.*

$ ✕ **Sticky Fingers.** Specializing in ribs six ways (Memphis-style wet and dry, Texas-style wet and dry, Carolina sweet, and Tennessee whiskey) and barbecue, this family-friendly restaurant has locations downtown and in Mount Pleasant and Summerville. Tuesday nights are kids' nights, with supervised games and cartoons in a playroom. ✉ *235 Meeting St.,* ☎ *803/853–7427 or 800/671–5966;* ✉ *U.S. 17*

Bypass, Mount Pleasant, ☎ *803/856–9840;* ✉ *1200 N. Main St., Summerville,* ☎ *803/875–7969. AE, DC, MC, V.*

Seafood

$$ ✕ **Barbadoes Room.** This large, airy plant- and light-filled space has a sophisticated island look and a view out to a cheery courtyard garden, where dinner may be served in warm weather, complete with a big band on Tuesday nights and jazz on Friday evenings. The menu includes she-crab soup; blackened shrimp and scallops; and oyster and crab gratin. The extensive breakfast buffet and Sunday brunch are popular, too. ✉ *115 Meeting St., in the Mills House Hotel,* ☎ *803/577–2400. Reservations essential. D, DC, MC, V.*

$ ✕ **The Wreck.** Dockside and full of wacky character, this spot serves up traditional dishes like boiled peanuts, fried shrimp, shrimp pilaf, deviled crab, and oyster platters in a shabby, candlelit, screened-in porch and small dining area. ✉ *106 Haddrell St., Mount Pleasant,* ☎ *803/884–0052. Reservations not accepted. No credit cards.*

LODGING

The charms of historic Charleston can be enhanced by a stay at one of its many inns, most in restored structures. Some are reminiscent of European inns; others are taste-fully contemporary. Rates tend to increase during the Spring Festival of Houses and Spoleto, when reservations are essential. The Charleston Area Convention and Visitors Bureau (✉ Box 975, Charleston 29402, ☎ 803/853–8000 or 800/868–8118) distributes a Visitor Value Days Card entitling the bearer to 10%–50% off at many accommodations between December 1 and March 1.

CATEGORY	COST*
$$$$	over $150
$$$	$90–$150
$$	$50–$90
$	under $50

All prices are for a standard double room, excluding 7% tax.

Hotels and Motels

$$$$ ☷ **Charleston Place.** Among the city's most luxurious ho-
★   tels—now an Orient Express property—this graceful, low-
rise structure in the historic district is surrounded by upscale
boutiques and specialty shops and ranked world-class. The
lobby has a magnificent hand-blown Venetian-glass chandelier, an Italian marble floor, and antiques from Sotheby's.
Rooms are furnished with period reproductions, linen
sheets and robes, and fax machines. ⊠ *130 Market St.,
29401,* ☎ *803/722–4900 or 800/611–5545,* ℻ *803/724–
7215. 400 rooms, 40 suites. 2 restaurants, 2 lounges, mini-
bars, indoor pool, hot tub, sauna, steam room, exercise
room, concierge floors. AE, D, DC, MC, V.*

$$$$ ☷ **Hawthorn Suites Hotel.** This deluxe hotel across from
the City Market includes a restored entrance portico from
an 1874 bank, a refurbished 1866 firehouse, and three
lush gardens. The spacious suites, all decorated with 18th-
century reproductions and canopied beds, have full kitchens
or wet bars with microwave ovens and refrigerators. Complimentary full breakfast and afternoon refreshments are
included. ⊠ *181 Church St., 29401,* ☎ *803/577–2644 or
800/527–1133,* ℻ *803/577–2697. 162 suites. Restaurant, lounge, hot tub, exercise room, business services,
meeting rooms. AE, D, DC, MC, V.*

$$$$ ☷ **Mills House Hotel.** Antique furnishings and period decor
★   give great charm to this luxurious Holiday Inn property, a
reconstruction of an old hostelry on its original site in the
historic district. Though rooms are small and a bit standard, there's a lounge with live entertainment and excellent dining in the **Barbadoes Room** (☞ Dining, *above*). ⊠
115 Meeting St., 29401, ☎ *803/577–2400 or 800/874–
9600,* ℻ *803/722–2712. 214 rooms, 15 suites. Restaurant,
2 lounges, pool. AE, D, DC, MC, V.*

$$$–   ☷ **Embassy Suites Historic Charleston.** The courtyard of the
$$$$ Old Citadel military school where cadets once marched is
now a skylit atrium with stone flooring, armchairs, palm
trees, and a fountain. The restored brick walls of the break-
fast room and some guest rooms in this new hotel contain
original gun ports, reminders that the 1822 building was
originally a fortification. Teak and mahogany furniture, sa-
fari motifs, and sisal carpeting recall the British colonial era.
⊠ *341 Meeting St., 29403,* ☎ *803/723–6900 or 800/*

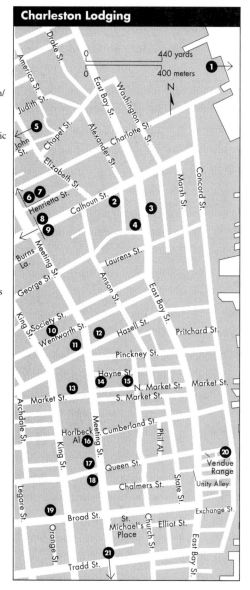

Charleston Lodging

362–2779, ✉ *803/723–6938. 153 suites. Lounge, pool, exercise room. AE, D, DC, MC, V.*

$$$– **🔲 Francis Marion Hotel.** Built in 1924 as the largest hotel
$$$$ in the Carolinas, this recently restored property retains big-band and tea-dance glamour with its windowed ballrooms, wrought-iron railings, columns, high ceilings, crown moldings, decorative plasterwork, and scenic views of Marion Square and the harbor (from some guest rooms you can see Fort Sumter). A few rooms have their original pedestal sinks and deep tubs. ✉ *387 King St., 29403,* ☎ *803/722–0600,* ✉ *803/723–4633. 160 rooms, 66 suites. Restaurant, lounge, exercise room. AE, D, DC, MC, V.*

$$–$$$ **🔲 Best Western King Charles Inn.** Renovated in 1997, this inn in the historic district is a cut above the typical chain, with a welcoming lobby and sitting area and spacious rooms furnished with 18th-century period reproductions. ✉ *237 Meeting St., 29401,* ☎ *803/723–7451 or 800/528–1234,* ✉ *803/723–2041. 91 rooms. Dining room, lounge, pool. AE, D, DC, MC, V.*

$$–$$$ **🔲 Days Inn Historic District.** Conveniently located, this modest property has spacious, quiet rooms and free parking. ✉ *155 Meeting St., 29401,* ☎ *803/722–8411 or 800/325–2525,* ✉ *803/733–5361. 124 rooms. Dining room, pool. AE, D, DC, MC, V.*

$$–$$$ **🔲 Hampton Inn–Historic District.** This downtown chain
★ offering has hardwood floors and a fireplace in the elegant lobby, guest rooms with period reproductions, a courtyard garden, and complimentary Continental breakfast. This is a front-runner in the economy category. ✉ *345 Meeting St., 29403,* ☎ *803/723–4000 or 800/426–7866,* ✉ *803/722–3725. 166 rooms, 5 suites. Pool. AE, D, DC, MC, V.*

$$–$$$ **🔲 Heart of Charleston Quality Inn.** A block from the Gaillard Municipal Auditorium and Exhibition Hall, the inn is clean and run by a friendly staff. It draws loyal repeat visitors because of its free parking and a location across from the auditorium that is within walking distance of many mustsee spots. Rooms are motel modern, as you would expect from this chain. ✉ *125 Calhoun St., 29401,* ☎ *803/722–3391 or 800/845–2504,* ✉ *803/577–0361. 126 rooms. Restaurant, lounge, pool. AE, D, DC, MC, V.*

$$–$$$　🏨 **Holiday Inn Charleston/Mount Pleasant.** This hotel just over the Cooper River Bridge is a 10-minute drive from the downtown historic district. Everything has been gracefully done: brass lamps, crystal chandeliers, Queen Anne–style furniture. The "high-tech suites" have PC cable hookups, large working areas, glossy ultramodern furniture, and refrigerators. ✉ *250 U.S. 17, Mount Pleasant 29464,* ☎ *803/884–6000 or 800/290–4004,* 🖷 *803/881–1786. 158 rooms. Restaurant, lounge, pool, sauna, exercise room, concierge floor, meeting rooms. AE, D, DC, MC, V.*

$$–$$$　🏨 **Sheraton Inn Charleston.** Some rooms in this 13-story hotel outside the historic district overlook the Ashley River. Spacious rooms and suites are furnished in Queen Anne style. There's also concierge service, live entertainment, and free shuttle service to the historic district. ✉ *170 Lockwood Dr., 29403,* ☎ *803/723–3000 or 800/968–3569,* 🖷 *803/720–0844. 333 rooms, 5 suites. Coffee shop, dining room, lounge, pool, exercise room, meeting rooms. AE, D, DC, MC, V.*

Inns and Guest Houses

$$$$　🏨 **John Rutledge House Inn.** This 1763 house, built by John
★　　Rutledge, one of the framers of the U.S. Constitution, is one of Charleston's most luxurious inns. Ornate ironwork on the facade has a palmetto tree and eagle motif, signifying Rutledge's service to both his state and his nation. A lavish afternoon tea, plus wine, is served in the ballroom, and Continental breakfast and newspapers are delivered to your room. Two charming period carriage houses also accommodate guests. There are whirlpool tubs in some guest rooms. ✉ *116 Broad St., 29401,* ☎ *803/723–7999 or 800/476–9741,* 🖷 *803/720–2615. 11 rooms in mansion, 4 in each of 2 carriage houses. In-room modem lines, business services. AE, DC, MC, V.*

$$$–　🏨 **Cannonboro Inn** and **Ashley Inn.** Two of the most ele-
$$$$　gant inns in town, these B&B neighbors on the edge of the historic district have luxurious rooms, tastefully decorated in period furnishings by owners Bud and Sally Allen. Guests are treated to a full English breakfast in piazzas overlooking Charleston gardens. Use of the bicycles, afternoon sherry, and convenient parking in an off-street lot are all included. *Cannonboro:* ✉ *184 Ashley Ave., 29403,* ☎ *803/723–8572,* 🖷 *803/723–9080. 6 rooms. Bicycles, busi-*

ness services. MC, V. Ashley: ⊠ *201 Ashley Ave., 29403,* ☎ *803/723–1848. 6 rooms, 1 suite. Bicycles, business services. MC, V.*

$$$–
$$$$ 🏨 **Planters Inn.** Rooms and suites are beautifully appointed with opulent furnishings, including mahogany four-poster beds and marble baths. Each of the 21 rooms in a new addition has a piazza overlooking the garden courtyard. The inn's Peninsula Grill (☞ Dining, *above*) is very popular. ⊠ *112 N. Market St., 29401,* ☎ *803/722–2345 or 800/845–7082,* ℻ *803/577–2125. 56 rooms, 6 suites. Restaurant, room service, concierge, business services. AE, D, DC, MC, V.*

$$$–
$$$$
★ 🏨 **Two Meeting Street.** As pretty as a wedding cake and just as romantic, this turn-of-the-century inn near the Battery has very private honeymoon suites. There are Tiffany windows, carved English oak paneling, and a chandelier from Czechoslovakia. Guests are treated to afternoon high tea and Continental breakfast. ⊠ *2 Meeting St., 29401,* ☎ *803/723–7322. 7 rooms, 2 suites. No credit cards.*

$$$–
$$$$ 🏨 **Vendue Inn.** Many rooms of this elegant yet friendly inn look out over the harbor and Waterfront Park. Guest rooms have four-poster beds, cozy seating areas, and large bathrooms. Continental breakfast plus afternoon wine and cheese are complimentary. Climb up to the inn's rooftop terrace bar for sweeping views of the harbor along with drinks and appetizers from the inn's Library Restaurant. ⊠ *19 Vendue Range, 29401,* ☎ *803/577–7970 or 800/845–7900. 21 suites. Restaurant, lounge, exercise room, business services, meeting rooms. AE, D, DC, MC, V.*

$$$ 🏨 **Ansonborough Inn.** Formerly a turn-of-the-century stationer's warehouse, this spacious all-suite inn is furnished in period reproductions. It offers hair dryers, irons, a morning newspaper, message service, wine reception, and Continental breakfast, but it's best known for its friendly staff. ⊠ *21 Hasell St., 29401,* ☎ *803/723–1655 or 800/522–2073,* ℻ *803/527–6888. 37 suites. Meeting room. AE, MC, V.*

$$$ 🏨 **Brasington House Bed & Breakfast.** During the afternoon wine-and-cheese get-together or at the family-style breakfast, Dalton and Judy Brasington, educators by profession, will advise you on what to see and do in Charleston. The formal dining room of their restored Greek Revival "single house" in the historic district is filled with antiques and treasures from around the world. ⊠ *328 E. Bay St., 29401,*

☎ *803/722–1274 or 800/722–1274*, 🖷 *803/722–6785.
4 rooms. MC, V.*

$$$ 🏨 **Elliott House Inn.** Listen to the chimes of St. Michael's
Episcopal Church as you sip wine in the courtyard of this
lovely old inn in the heart of the historic district. You can
then retreat to a cozy room with period furniture, includ-
ing canopied four-posters and Oriental carpets. A Conti-
nental breakfast is included. ✉ *78 Queen St., 29401,* ☎
803/723–1855 or 800/729–1855, 🖷 *803/722–1567. 26
rooms. Hot tub, bicycles. AE, D, MC, V.*

$$$ 🏨 **Maison DuPré.** A quiet retreat off busy East Bay Street,
this inn was created out of three restored homes and two
carriage houses. It is filled with antiques, and each room
contains an original painting by Lucille Mullholland, who
operates the inn with her husband, Robert. Enjoy a full Lowcountry tea (with cheeses, finger sandwiches, and cakes) and
Continental breakfast, all complimentary. ✉ *317 E. Bay
St., 29401,* ☎ *803/723–8691 or 800/844–4667. 12 rooms,
3 suites. MC, V.*

$$–$$$ 🏨 **1837 Bed and Breakfast and Tea Room.** Though not as
fancy as some of the B&Bs in town, this inn is long on hospitality; you'll get a sense of what it's really like to live in
one of Charleston's beloved homes. Restored and operated
by two artists/teachers, the home and carriage house have
rooms filled with antiques, including romantic canopied beds.
A gourmet breakfast of homemade breads and hot entrées
such as sausage pie or ham frittata is included in the rate,
as is the afternoon tea (which is also open to the public for
a nominal price). ✉ *126 Wentworth St., 29401,* ☎ *803/
723–7166. 8 rooms. AE, MC, V.*

Resort Islands

The semitropical islands dotting the South Carolina coast
near Charleston are home to several sumptuous resorts
that offer a wide variety of packages. Peak season rates (during spring and summer vacations) range from $100 to
$250 per day, double occupancy. Costs drop considerably
off-season.

$$$$ ✕🏨 **Kiawah Island Resort.** Choose from 150 inn rooms and
500 completely equipped one- to five-bedroom villas and

private homes in two luxurious resort villages on 10,000 wooded acres. There are 10 mi of fine broad beaches and an array of recreational opportunities. Dining options are many and varied. At press time the resort planned to demolish the inn and build a larger hotel, but the rest of the resort will remain open. ⊠ *12 Kiawah Beach Dr., Kiawah Island 29455,* ☎ *803/768–2121 or 800/654–2924,* ℻ *803/768–6099. 150 rooms, 500 villa and private homes. 8 restaurants, 4 18-hole golf courses, 28 tennis courts, boating, fishing, bicycles, shops, children's programs. AE, D, DC, MC, V.*

$$$$ ✕⚼ **Seabrook Island Resort.** A total of 175 completely equipped one- to three-bedroom villas, cottages, and beach houses dot this property. The **Beach Club** and **Island Club,** open to all guests, are centers for dining and leisure activities. **Bohicket Marina Village,** the hub of activity around the island, offers three fine restaurants as well as pizza and sub shops. The marina area includes opportunities for shopping as well as scuba diving, deep sea and inshore fishing charters, and small-boat rentals. ⊠ *1002 Landfall Way, Seabrook Island 29455,* ☎ *803/768–1000 or 800/845–2475,* ℻ *803/768–4946. 175 units. 3 restaurants, 2 pools, 2 18-hole golf courses, 13 tennis courts, horseback riding, boating, parasailing, fishing, bicycles, children's programs. AE, D, DC, MC, V.*

$$$$ ✕⚼ **Wild Dunes.** This serene, 1,600-acre resort on the Isle of Palms has 300 one- to three-bedroom villas for rent, each with a kitchen and washer and dryer. Rooms at the new **Inn at Wild Dunes** are another option. There are two widely acclaimed golf courses, a racquet club, a yacht harbor on the Intracoastal Waterway, and a long list of recreational options. Southern regional specialties are served at **Edgar's,** seafood at the **Tradewinds Restaurant,** and casual fare at the **Dune Deli and Pizzeria.** There's a lounge with live entertainment. ⊠ *Box 20575, Charleston 29413,* ☎ *803/886–6000 or 800/845–8880,* ℻ *803/886–2916. 300 units, 93 rooms. 3 restaurants, lounge, 2 18-hole golf courses, 17 tennis courts, health club, water sports, boating, fishing, bicycles, rollerblading, children's programs. AE, MC, DC, D, V.*

NIGHTLIFE AND THE ARTS

Concerts

The College of Charleston has a free **Monday Night Recital Series** (☎ 803/953–8228).

The **Charleston Symphony Orchestra** (☎ 803/723–7528) presents MasterWorks Series, Downtown Pops, First Union Family Series, and Annual Holiday Concert at Gaillard Municipal Auditorium (✉ 77 Calhoun St., ☎ 803/577–4500). The orchestra also performs the Sotille Chamber Series at the **Sotille Theater** (✉ 44 George St., ☎ 803/953–6340), and the Light and Lively Pops at Charleston Southern University (✉ U.S. 78, ☎ 803/953–6340).

The **Charleston Concert Association** (☎ 803/722–7667) presents visiting performing arts groups including symphonies, ballets, and operas.

Dance

The **Charleston Ballet Theatre** (✉ 477 King St., ☎ 803/723–7334) performs everything from classical to contemporary dance at locations around the city.

The **Robert Ivey Ballet Company** (☎ 803/556–1343), a semiprofessional company that includes several College of Charleston students, gives a fall and spring program of jazz, classical, and modern dance at the Sotille Theater.

Anonymity Dance Company (☎ 803/886–6104 or 800/215–6523), a modern dance troupe, performs throughout the city.

Dancing and Music

Lowcountry Legends Music Hall (✉ 30 Cumberland St., ☎ 803/722–1829 or 800/348–7270) is Charleston's Preservation Hall, serving up regional music and folktales.

Serenade (✉ 37 John St., ☎ 803/973–3333), a 1,000-seat music hall, showcases jazz, blues, calypso, Broadway tunes, and more in the city's only revue.

The **Music Farm** (⊠ 32 Ann St., ☎ 803/853–3276) features live national and local alternative bands.

In the market area, there's the **Jukebox** (⊠ 4 Vendue Range, ☎ 803/723–3431), where a disc jockey spins oldies and contemporary rock.

The **Chef & Clef Restaurant** (⊠ 102 N. Market St., ☎ 803/722–0732) has jazz on one floor and the Red Hot Blues room on another.

Windjammer (⊠ 1000 Ocean Blvd., ☎ 803/886–8596), on the Isle of Palms, is an oceanfront spot with live rock.

Dinner Cruises

For an evening of dining and dancing, climb aboard the luxury yacht, **Spirit of Charleston** (☎ 803/722–2628). Reservations are essential; there are no cruises Sunday and Monday.

Breakfast, brunch, deli and hot luncheons are available and prepared freshly on board the **Charlestowne Princess** (☎ 803/722–1112), which also offers a "Harborlites Dinner" with live entertainment and dancing while cruising the harbor and rivers.

Festivals

The **Fall Candelight Tours of Homes and Gardens** (⊠ Box 521, 29402, ☎ 803/722–4630), sponsored by the Preservation Society of Charleston in September and October, offers an inside look at Charleston's private buildings and gardens.

During the **Festival of Houses and Gardens** (⊠ Box 1120, 29202, ☎ 803/724–8484), held during March and April each year, more than 100 private homes, gardens, and historic churches are open to the public for tours sponsored by the Historic Charleston Foundation. There are also symphony galas in stately drawing rooms, plantation oyster roasts, and candlelight tours.

MOJA Arts Festival (⊠ Office of Cultural Affairs, 133 Church St., 29401, ☎ 803/724–7305), which takes place during the last week of September and first week of October, celebrates the rich heritage of the African continent and Caribbean influences on African-American culture. It includes theater, dance, and music performances, art shows, films, lectures, and tours of the historic district.

Piccolo Spoleto Festival (⊠ Office of Cultural Affairs, 133 Church St., 29401, ☎ 803/724–7305) is the spirited companion festival of Spoleto Festival USA, showcasing the best in local and regional talent from every artistic discipline. There are about 300 events—from jazz performances to puppet shows—held at 60 sites in 17 days, from mid-May through early June, and most performances are free.

The **Southeastern Wildlife Exposition** (⊠ 211 Meeting St., 29401, ☎ 803/723–1748 or 800/221–5273) in mid-February is one of Charleston's biggest annual events. It features art by renowned wildlife artists.

Spoleto Festival USA (⊠ Box 704, 29402, ☎ 803/722–2764), founded by the composer Gian Carlo Menotti in 1977, has become a world-famous celebration of the arts. For two weeks, from late May to early June, opera, dance, theater, symphonic and chamber music performances, jazz, and the visual arts are showcased in concert halls, theaters, parks, churches, streets, and gardens throughout the city.

The reasonably priced **Worldfest Charleston** (⊠ Box 838, 29402, ☎ 803/723–7600 or 800/501–0111), held in mid-November, premieres new films from around the world, offers workshops and seminars, and provides opportunities to meet the producers, directors, and actors.

Film

The **Roxy** (⊠ 245 E. Bay St., ☎ 803/853–7699) offers films from around the world plus wine, beer, coffee drinks, pastries, sandwiches, and pasta.

The **American Theater** (⊠ 446 King St., ☎ 803/722–3456), a renovated theater from the 1940s, shows second-run movies in a table-and-chairs setting with pizza, burgers, finger foods, beer, and wine. Upstairs there's a virtual reality game center.

Hotel and Jazz Bars

The **Best Friend Lounge** (✉ 115 Meeting St., ☎ 803/577–2400), in the Mills House Hotel, has a guitarist playing light tunes Monday–Saturday nights.

In the **Lobby Lounge** (✉ 130 Market St., ☎ 803/722–4900) in Charleston Place, cocktails and appetizers are accompanied by piano.

Charlie's Little Bar, above the Saracen Restaurant (✉ 141 E. Bay St., ☎ 803/723–6242), has live jazz or blues most weekends.

Live jazz is offered Friday and Saturday evenings at **Henry's Restaurant** (✉ 54 N. Market St., ☎ 803/723–4363).

Lounges and Bars/Breweries

The bustling **Kiva Han Cafe & Coffee House** (✉ 235 E. Bay St., ☎ 803/965–5282) has live music plus late-night food and drink.

Southend Brewery (✉ 161 E. Bay St., ☎ 803/853–4677) has a lively bar with beer brewed on the premises; the food is good, especially soups.

Zebo (✉ 275 King St., ☎ 803/577–7600) brews its beer here and offers tasty meals.

Vickery's Bar & Grill (✉ 139 Calhoun St., ☎ 803/723–1558) is a festive night spot with a spacious outdoor patio.

You'll find authentic Irish music at **Tommy Condon's Irish Pub & Restaurant** (✉ 160 Church St., ☎ 803/577–3818).

Club Habana (✉ 177 Meeting St., ☎ 803/853–5900) is a fancy, wood-paneled martini bar with a cigar shop downstairs.

Theater

Several groups, including the **Footlight Players** and **Charleston Stage Company,** perform at the Dock Street Theatre (✉ 135 Church St., ☎ 803/723–5648).

Performances by the College of Charleston's theater department and guest theatrical groups are presented during the school year at the **Simons Center for the Arts** (⊠ 54 St. Phillips St., ☎ 803/953–5604).

Pluff Mud Productions puts on comedies at the Isle of Palms' Windjammer (1000 Ocean Blvd., ☎ 803/886-8596).

The **Cavallaro** (⊠ 1478 Savannah Hwy., ☎ 803/763–9222) is the home of several successful dinner theater productions.

OUTDOOR ACTIVITIES AND SPORTS

Beaches

The Charleston area's mild climate generally is conducive to swimming from April through October. This is definitely not a "swingles" area; all public and private beaches are family oriented, providing a choice of water sports, sunbathing, shelling, fishing, or quiet moonlight strolls. The **Charleston County Parks and Recreation Commission** (☎ 803/762–2172) operates several public beach facilities.

Beachwalker Park on the west end of Kiawah Island (which is otherwise a private resort) provides 300 ft of beach frontage, seasonal lifeguard service, rest rooms, outdoor showers, a picnic area, snack bar, and a 150-car parking lot. ⊠ *Kiawah Island,* ☎ *803/762–2172.* ▨ *$4 per car (up to 8 passengers).* ☉ *June–Aug., daily 10–7; Apr. and Oct., weekends 10–6; May and Sept., daily 10–6.*

Folly Beach County Park, 12 mi south of Charleston via U.S. 17 and SC 171 (Folly Rd.), has 4,000 ft of ocean frontage and 2,000 ft of river frontage. Lifeguards are on duty seasonally along a 600-ft section of the beach. Facilities include dressing areas, outdoor showers, rest rooms, picnicking areas, beach chairs, raft and shower rentals, and a 300-vehicle parking lot. Pelican Watch shelter is available year-round for group picnics and day or night oyster roasts. ⊠ *Folly Island,* ☎ *803/588–2426.* ▨ *$4 per car (up to 8 pas-*

sengers). ☉ *May–Aug., daily 9–7; Apr., Sept., Oct., 10–6; Nov.–Mar., daily 10–5.*

Private resorts with extensive beaches and amenities include **Fairfield Ocean Ridge** (☎ 803/869–2561), on Edisto Island; **Kiawah Island** (☎ 903/768–2121 or 800/654–2924); **Seabrook Island** (☎ 803/768–1000 or 800/845–5531); and **Wild Dunes** (☎ 803/886–6000 or 800/845–8880), on the Isle of Palms.

Participant Sports

Biking

The historic district is ideal for bicycling, and many city parks have biking trails. Palmetto Islands County Park (☞ Mount Pleasant and Vicinity, *above*) also has trails.

Bikes can be rented at the **Bicycle Shoppe** (✉ 280 Meeting St., ☎ 803/722–8168; ✉ Kiawah Island, ☎ 803/768–9122).

Sea Island Cycle (✉ 4053 Rhett Ave., North Charleston, ☎ 803/747–2453) serves all the local islands.

Island Bike and Surf Shop (✉ 3665 Bohicket Rd., Kiawah Island, ☎ 803/768–1158) has bikes, surfboards, and rollerblades for rent.

Golf

One of the most appealing aspects of golfing the Charleston area is the relaxing pace. With fewer golfers playing the courses than in destinations that are primarily golf-oriented, golfers find choice starting times and an unhurried atmosphere. For a listing of area golf packages, contact the Charleston Area Convention and Visitors Bureau (✉ Box 975, 29402, ☎ 803/853–8000 or 800/868–8118).

Nonguests may play on a space-available basis at **private island resorts** such as Kiawah Island, Seabrook Island, and Wild Dunes. The prestigious Pete Dye–designed **Ocean Course at Kiawah Island Resort** (☎ 803/768–7272) was the site of the 1991 Ryder Cup. Other championship **Kiawah courses** are the Gary Player–designed **Marsh Point; Osprey Point,** by Tom Fazio; and **Turtle Point,** a Jack Nicklaus layout (☎ 803/768–2121 for all three). **Seabrook**

Island Resort, a secluded hideaway on Johns Island, offers two more championship courses: **Crooked Oaks** by Robert Trent Jones Sr., and **Ocean Winds,** designed by William Byrd (☎ 803/768–2529 for both). **Wild Dunes Resort,** on the Isle of Palms, is home to two Tom Fazio designs: the **Links** (☎ 803/886–2180) and **Harbor Course** (☎ 803/886–2301).

Top **public courses** in the area include **Charleston Municipal** (☎ 803/795–6517), **Charleston National Country Club** (☎ 803/884–7799), the **Dunes West Golf Club** (✉ Mount Pleasant, ☎ 803/856–9000), **Links at Stono Ferry** (✉ Hollywood, ☎ 803/763–1817), **Oak Point Golf Course** (✉ Johns Island, ☎ 803/768–7431), **Patriots Point** (✉ Mount Pleasant, ☎ 803/881–0042), and **Shadowmoss Golf Club** (☎ 803/556–8251).

Tennis

Courts are open to the public at **Shadowmoss Plantation** (☎ 803/556–8251), **Kiawah Island** (☎ 803/768–2121), and **Wild Dunes** (☎ 803/886–6000).

Spectator Sports

Baseball

The minor-league **RiverDogs** (✉ 360 Fishburne St., ☎ 803/723–7241) play at the Joseph P. Riley Jr. Ballpark from April through August.

Hockey

The Charleston **Stingrays** (✉ 3107 Firestone Rd., North Charleston, ☎ 803/747–2248), ranked first in the East Coast Hockey League, play at the North Charleston Coliseum to record-breaking crowds from October through March.

SHOPPING

Shopping Districts

The Market is a complex of specialty shops and restaurants. Don't miss the colorful produce market in the three-block **Old City Market** (✉ E. Bay and Market Sts.) and, adjacent to it, the open-air flea market, with crafts, antiques, and memorabilia. You'll find locally produced sweetgrass and other baskets here. Other such complexes in the historic district are the **Shops at Charleston Place** (⊠ 130 Market St.) and **Rainbow Market** (⊠ 40 N. Market St.), in two interconnected 150-year-old buildings; **Market Square;** and **State Street Market** (⊠ 67 State St.). **King Street** has some of Charleston's oldest and finest shops, along with the new Saks Fifth Avenue (⊠ 211 King St., ☎ 803/853–9888). From May until September, the festive **Farmer's Market** takes place each Saturday morning in Marion Square.

Antiques

Petterson Antiques (⊠ 201 King St., ☎ 803/723–5714) offers curious objets d'art, books, furniture, porcelain, and glass.

Livingston & Sons Antiques, dealers in 18th- and 19th-century English and Continental furniture, clocks, and bric-a-brac, has a large shop west of the Ashley (⊠ 2137 Savannah Hwy., ☎ 803/556–6162) and a smaller one on King (⊠ 163 King St., ☎ 803/723–9697).

Birlant & Co. (⊠ 191 King St., ☎ 803/722–3842) presents fine 18th- and 19th-century English antiques, as well as the famous Charleston Battery bench, identical to those on Charleston Green.

Art and Craft Galleries

The **Birds I View Gallery** (⊠ 119–A Church St., ☎ 803/723–1276) sells bird paintings and prints by Anne Worsham Richardson.

Birds & Ivy (⊠ 235 King St., ☎ 803/853–8534), which sells garden art and accessories of every type, also has a café in back.

Charleston Crafts (⊠ 38 Queen St., ☎ 803/723–2938) has a fine selection of pottery, quilts, weavings, sculptures, and jewelry fashioned mostly by local artists.

The **Elizabeth O'Neill Verner Studio & Museum** (⊠ 79 Church St., ☎ 803/722–4246), in a 17th-century house, is open to the public. Prints of Elizabeth O'Neill Verner's pastels and etchings are on sale at the adjacent **Tradd Street Press** (⊠ 38 Tradd St., ☎ 803/722–4246).

The **Marty Whaley Adams Gallery** (✉ 120 Meeting St., ☎ 803/853–8512) has original vivid watercolors and mono-types, plus prints and posters by this Charleston artist.

At **Nina Liu and Friends** (✉ 24 State St., ☎ 803/722–2724), you'll find contemporary art objects including hand-blown glass, pottery, jewelry, and photographs.

The **Virginia Fouché Bolton Art Gallery** (✉ 127 Meeting St., ☎ 803/577–9351) sells original paintings and limited-edition lithographs of Charleston and Lowcountry scenes.

Books

Chapter Two (✉ 199 E. Bay St., ☎ 803/722–4238), an independently owned, unique little nook, specializes in local and regional books; there's also a neat section for kids.

The **Preservation Society of Charleston** (✉ Corner of King and Queen Sts., ☎ 803/722–4630) has books and tapes of historic and local interest, sweetgrass baskets, prints, and posters.

Gifts

Charleston Collections (✉ 233 King St., ☎ 803/722–7267; ✉ Straw Market, Kiawah Island Resort, ☎ 803/768–7487; ✉ Quadrangle Center, ☎ 803/556–8911) has Charleston chimes, prints, candies, T-shirts, and more.

Charleston's and London's own **Ben Silver** (✉ 149 King St., ☎ 803/577–4556), premier purveyor of blazer buttons, has over 800 designs, including college and British regimental motifs. He also sells British neckties, embroidered polo shirts, and blazers.

Period Reproductions

Historic Charleston Reproductions (✉ 105 Broad St., ☎ 803/723–8292) has superb replicas of Charleston furniture and accessories, all authorized by the Historic Charleston Foundation. Royalties from sales contribute to restoration projects.

At the **Old Charleston Joggling Board Co.** (✉ 652 King St., ☎ 803/723–4331), these Lowcountry oddities (on which people bounce) can be purchased.

SIDE TRIPS FROM CHARLESTON

Gardens, parks, and the charming town of Summerville are good reasons to travel a bit farther afield for some day trips.

Moncks Corner

30 mi north of Charleston on U.S. 52.

This town is a gateway to a number of attractions. Here in Santee Cooper Country, named for the two rivers that form a 171,000-acre basin, the area brims with outdoor pleasures centered around the basin and nearby Lakes Marion and Moultrie.

Cypress Gardens, a swamp garden created from what was once the freshwater reserve of the vast Dean Hall rice plantation, is about 24 mi north of Charleston via U.S. 52, between Goose Creek and Moncks Corner. Explore the inky waters by boat, or walk along paths lined with moss-draped cypress trees, azaleas, camellias, daffodils, wisteria, and dogwood. ✉ *3030 Cypress Gardens Rd.,* ☎ *803/ 553–0515.* ✍ *$5 (Mar.–Apr. $6).* ☉ *Daily 9–5.*

On the banks of the Old Santee Canal is the ☾ **Old Santee Canal State Park,** reached via I–26 and U.S. 52. You can explore on foot or take a canoe. There's also an interpretive center. ✉ *Rembert C. Dennis Blvd.,* ☎ *803/899– 5200.* ✍ *$3 per car.* ☉ *Daily 9–6; spring and summer weekends 9–7.*

Francis Marion National Forest consists of 250,000 acres of swamps, vast oaks and pines, and little lakes thought to have been formed by falling meteors. It's a good place for picnicking, camping, boating, and swimming. At the park's **Rembert Dennis Wildlife Center** (✉ Off U.S. 52 in Bonneau, north of Moncks Corner, ☎ 803/825–3387), deer, wild turkey, and striped bass are reared and studied. ✉ *35 mi north of Charleston via U.S. 52,* ☎ *803/336–3248.* ✍ *Free.*

Fishing

Lakes Marion and **Moultrie** are full of bream, striped bass, catfish, and large- and smallmouth bass. For information, contact Santee Cooper Counties Promotion Commission (✉ Drawer 40, Santee 29142, ☎ 803/854–2131; 800/227–8510 outside South Carolina).

Summerville

25 mi northwest of Charleston via I–26 (Exit 199), SC 78, or SC 61 and SC 165.

Built by wealthy planters as an escape from hot-weather malaria, this picturesque town is a treasure trove of Victorian buildings, many of which are listed in the National Register of Historic Places. Colorful gardens of camellias, azaleas, and wisteria abound, and many streets curve around tall pines, as a local ordinance prohibits cutting them down. This is a good place for a bit of antiquing in attractive shops. To get oriented, stop by the **Summerville Chamber of Commerce** (✉ 106 E. Doty Ave., Box 670, 29483, ☎ 803/873–2931). It's open weekdays 8:30–12:30 and 1:30–5, Saturday 10–3.

Dining and Lodging

$$$$ ✕▦ **Woodlands Inn.** People drive from Charleston for su-
★ perb meals at this luxury inn's restaurant ($$$–$$$$), which recently joined the prestigious Relais & Châteaux group. There's a three-course ($38) or four-course ($44) menu, plus a more expensive chef's tasting menu. Delicate sauces and subtle touches are key in entrées such as Angus beef with celery root home fries and Barolo wine reduction, and soft-shell crab with doubloon mushrooms, lemon grass, and ginger. Though the inn, built in 1906 as a winter home, backs up to a suburb, it's a first-rate getaway with such niceties as fireplaces and whirlpool or claw-foot tubs. Breakfast is included in the rate, as is a split of champagne at arrival and afternoon tea. ✉ *125 Parsons Rd., 29483, ☎ 803/875–2600 or 800/774–9999, 𝖥𝖠𝖷 803/875–2603. 16 rooms, 4 suites. Restaurant, lounge, pool, spa, 2 tennis courts, croquet, bicycles. AE, D, DC, MC, V.*

CHARLESTON A TO Z

Arriving and Departing

By Boat

Boaters on the Intracoastal Waterway may dock at **City Marina** (⊠ Lockwood Blvd., ☎ 803/724–7357) in Charleston Harbor or **Wild Dunes Yacht Harbor** (☎ 803/886–5100) on the Isle of Palms.

By Bus

Greyhound (⊠ 3610 Dorchester Rd., N. Charleston, ☎ 800/231–2222).

By Car

I–26 traverses the state from northwest to southeast and terminates at Charleston. U.S. 17, the coast road, passes through Charleston.

By Plane

Charleston International Airport (☎ 803/767–1100) on I–26, 12 mi west of downtown, is served by Air South, Continental, Delta, Midway Connection, United, and US Airways.

Lowcountry Limousine Service (☎ 803/767–7111 or 800/222–4771) charges $15 per person (or $10 per person for two or more) to downtown. If you're traveling from the airport by **car,** take I–26S into the city.

By Train

Amtrak (⊠ 4565 Gaynor Ave., N. Charleston, ☎ 803/744–8264 or 800/872–7245).

Getting Around

By Boat

CHARTS (⊠ 196A Concord, ☎ 803/853–4700) is the only full-service water taxi providing transportation to and from Patriots Point naval and maritime museum. It also offers harbor cruises.

By Bus

Regular buses run in most of Charleston from 5:35 AM until 10 PM and to North Charleston until 1 AM. The cost is 75¢

exact change (free transfers). DASH (Downtown Area Shuttle) trolley-style buses provide fast service in the main downtown areas. The fare is 75¢; $2 for an all-day pass. For schedule information, call 803/747–0922.

By Taxi

Fares within the city average $2–$3 per trip. Companies include **Yellow Cab** (☎ 803/577–6565), **Safety Cab** (☎ 803/722–4066), and **Lowcountry Limousine Service** (☞ Arriving and Departing, *above*).

Contacts and Resources

Emergencies

Police (☎ 911). **Ambulance** (☎ 911). The **emergency rooms** are open all night at Charleston Memorial Hospital (✉ 326 Calhoun St., ☎ 803/577–0600) and Roper Hospital (✉ 316 Calhoun St., ☎ 803/724–2000).

Guided Tours

Princess Gray Line Harbor Tours (☎ 803/722–1112 or 800/344–4483) and **Charleston Harbor Tour** (☎ 803/722–1691) ply the harbor. **Fort Sumter Tours** (☎ 803/722–1691) includes a stop at Fort Sumter and also offers Starlight Dinner Cruises aboard a luxury yacht. **Flying High Over Charleston** (☎ 803/569–6148) provides aerial tours. **Adventure Sightseeing** (☎ 803/762–0088 or 800/722–5394) and **Colonial Coach and Trolley Company** (☎ 803/795–3000) offer motor-coach tours of the historic district. **Gray Line** (☎ 803/722–4444) offers tours of the historic district, plus seasonal trips to gardens and plantations.

Charleston Carriage Co. (☎ 803/577–0042), **Old South Carriage Company** (☎ 803/723–9712), and **Palmetto Carriage Works** (☎ 803/723–8145) run approximately one-hour horse- and mule-drawn carriage tours of the historic district, some conducted by guides in Confederate uniforms. **Doin' the Charleston** (☎ 803/763–1233 or 800/647–4487), a van tour, combines its narration with audiovisuals and makes a stop at the Battery.

Chai Y'All (☎ 803/556–0664) shares stories and sites of Jewish interest. **Sweet Grass Tours** (☎ 803/556–0664 for groups) focus on African-American influences on Charleston architecture, history, and culture.

Walking tours are given by **Historic Charleston Walking Tours** (☏ 803/722–6460); **Charleston Strolls** (☏ 803/884–9505); **Architectural Walking Tours of Charleston** (☏ 803/893–2327); and **Charleston Tea Party Walking Tour** (☏ 803/577–5896 or 803/722–1779), which includes tea in a private garden. For a spookier view of the city, take the **Ghosts of Charleston** (☏ 803/723–1670 or 800/854–1670) walking tour. The same guides also celebrate the city in the Story of Charleston walking tour.

Late-Night Pharmacies
Henry's Conway Drug Store (⊠ 517 King St., ☏ 803/577–5123). **Tellis Pharmacy** (⊠ 125 King St., ☏ 803/723–0682). **Eckerds** (⊠ 466 Savannah Hwy., ☏ 803/766–5593).

Lodging Assistance
Rates tend to increase during the Spring Festival of Houses and Spoleto, when reservations are essential. To find rooms in homes, cottages, and carriage houses, try **Historic Charleston Bed and Breakfast** (⊠ 60 Broad St., Charleston 29401, ☏ 803/722–6606). **Southern Hospitality B&B Reservations** (⊠ 110 Amelia Dr., Lexington 29072, ☏ 803/356–6238 or 800/374–7422) handles rooms in homes and carriage houses. For historic home rentals in Charleston, contact **Charleston Carriage Houses–Oceanfront Realty** (⊠ Box 6151, Hilton Head 29938, ☏ 803/785–8161). For condo and house rentals on the Isle of Palms—some with private pools and tennis courts—try **Island Realty** (⊠ Box 157, Isle of Palms 29451, ☏ 803/886–8144).

Personal Guides
Contact **Associated Guides of Historic Charleston** (☏ 803/724–6419); **Cary Parker Limousine Service** (☏ 803/723–7601), which offers chauffeur-driven luxury limousine tours; or **Charleston Guide Service** (☏ 803/722–8240), the city's oldest guide service. **Janice Kahn** (☏ 803/556–0664) has done individualized guiding for 25 years.

Radio Stations
AM: WQIZ 810, gospel; WTMA 1250, talk radio; WXTC 1390, sports. **FM:** WBUB 107.5, country; WJZK 96.9, smooth jazz; WSCI 89.3, news, classical, jazz, information

line; WWWZ 93.4, urban contemporary; WYBB 98.1, classic rock.

Telephones

The area code for Charleston will change from 803 to 843 in September, 1998.

Visitor Information

You can pick up the Schedule of Events at the Visitors Center (✉ 375 Meeting St.) or at area hotels, inns, and restaurants. Also see "Tips for Tourists" each Saturday in the *Post & Courier.* **Charleston Area Convention and Visitors Bureau** (✉ Box 975, Charleston 29402, ☎ 803/853–8000 or 800/868–8118) has information on the city and also on Kiawah Island, Seabrook Island, Mount Pleasant, North Charleston, Edisto Island, Summerville, and the Isle of Palms. **Historic Charleston Foundation** (✉ Box 1120, Charleston 29402, ☎ 803/723–1623) and the **Preservation Society of Charleston** (✉ Box 521, 29402, ☎ 803/722–4630) have information on house tours.

5 *Midnight in the Garden of Good and Evil—* An Excerpt

By John
Berendt

THERE BEING no direct route to Savannah from Charleston, I followed a zigzagging course that took me through the tidal flatlands of the South Carolina low country. As I approached Savannah, the road narrowed to a two-lane blacktop shaded by tall trees. There was an occasional produce stand by the side of the road and a few cottages set into the foliage, but nothing resembling urban sprawl. The voice on the car radio informed me that I had entered a zone called the Coastal Empire. "The weather outlook for the Coastal Empire," it said, "is for highs in the mid-eighties, with moderate seas and a light chop on the inland waters."

Abruptly, the trees gave way to an open panorama of marsh grass the color of wheat. Straight ahead, a tall bridge rose steeply out of the plain. From the top of the bridge, I looked down on the Savannah River and, on the far side, a row of old brick buildings fronted by a narrow esplanade. Behind the buildings a mass of trees extended into the distance, punctuated by steeples, cornices, rooftops, and cupolas. As I descended from the bridge, I found myself plunging into a luxuriant green garden.

Walls of thick vegetation rose up on all sides and arched overhead in a lacy canopy that filtered the light to a soft shade. It had just rained; the air was hot and steamy. I felt enclosed in a semitropical terrarium, sealed off from a world that suddenly seemed a thousand miles away.

The streets were lined with townhouses of brick and stucco, handsome old buildings with high front stoops and shuttered windows. I entered a square that had flowering shrubs and a monument at the center. A few blocks farther on, there was another square. Up ahead, I could see a third on line with this one, and a fourth beyond that. To the left and right, there were two more squares. There were squares in every direction. I counted eight of them. Ten. Fourteen. Or was it twelve?

"There are exactly twenty-one squares," an elderly lady told me later in the afternoon. Her name was Mary Harty. Acquaintances in Charleston had put us in touch; she had been expecting me. She had white hair and arched eyebrows that gave her a look of permanent surprise. We stood in her kitchen while she mixed martinis in a silver shaker. When she was finished, she put the shaker into a wicker basket. She was going to take me on an excursion, she said. It was too nice a day, and I had too little time in Savannah for us to waste it indoors.

As far as Miss Harty was concerned, the squares were the jewels of Savannah. No other city in the world had anything like them. There were five on Bull Street, five on Barnard, four on Abercorn, and so on. James Oglethorpe, the founder of Georgia, had been responsible for them, she said. He had decided Savannah was going to be laid out with squares, based on the design of a Roman military encampment, even before he set sail from England—before he even knew exactly where on the map he was going to put Savannah. When he arrived in February 1733, he chose a site for the city on top of a forty-foot bluff on the southern bank of the Savannah River, eighteen miles inland from the Atlantic. He had already sketched out the plans. The streets were to be laid out in a grid pattern, crossing at right angles, and there would be squares at regular intervals. In effect, the city would become a giant parterre garden. Oglethorpe built the first four squares himself. "The thing I like best about the squares," Miss Harty said, "is that cars can't cut through the middle; they must go *around* them. So traffic is obliged to flow at a very leisurely pace. The squares are our little oases of tranquillity."

As she spoke, I recognized in her voice the coastal accent described in *Gone with the Wind*—"soft and slurring, liquid of vowels, kind to consonants."

"But actually," she said, "the whole of Savannah is an oasis. We are isolated. Gloriously isolated! We're a little enclave on the coast—off by ourselves, surrounded by nothing but marshes and piney woods. We're not easy to get to at all, as you may have noticed . . ..Cities all around us are booming urban centers: Charleston, Atlanta, Jacksonville-but not Savannah. The Prudential Insurance people wanted to locate their regional headquarters here in the nineteen-fifties. It would have created thousands of jobs and made

Savannah an important center of a nice, profitable, non-polluting industry. But we said no. Too big. They gave it to Jacksonville instead. In the nineteen-seventies, Gian Carlo Menotti considered making Savannah the permanent home for his Spoleto U.S.A. Festival. Again, we were not interested. So Charleston go it. It's not that we're trying to be difficult. We just happen to like things exactly the way they are!"

Miss Harty opened a cupboard and took out two silver goblets. She wrapped each of them in a linen napkin and placed them carefully in the wicker basket beside the martinis.

"We may be standoffish," she said, "but we're not hostile. We're famously hospitable, in fact, even by southern standards. Savannah's called the 'Hostess City of the South,' you know. That's because we've always been a party town. We love company. We always have. I suppose that comes from being a port city and having played host to people from far-away places for so long. Life in Savannah was always easier than it was out on the plantations. Savannah was a city of rich cotton traders, who lived in elegant houses within strolling distance of one another. Parties became a way of life, and it's made a difference. We're not at all like the rest of Georgia. We have a saying: If you go to Atlanta, the first question people ask you is, 'What's your business?' In Macon they ask, 'Where do you go to church?' In Augusta they ask your grandmother's maiden name. But in Savannah the first question people ask you is 'What would you like to drink?'"

INDEX

✕ = *restaurant*, ⊞ = *hotel*

sports, 96–98
telephones, 106
transportation, 103–104
visitor information, 106
Charleston Museum, 66, 69
Charleston Place 🏨, 7, 68, 70, 85
Chatham County Courthouse, 23, 24
Chippewa Square, 12, 15
Christ Episcopal Church, 56
Churches
Charleston, 66, 68, 70, 71, 74
St. Simons Island, 56
Savannah, 14, 15, 16, 20, 25–26
Circular Congregational Church, 68, 70
City Hall (Charleston), 68, 70
City Hall (Savannah), 12, 15
City Market, 12, 15
Civil War sites, 5–6, 26, 28, 72, 76–77
CJ's ✕, 56
Clamagore (submarine), 77
Climate, *xx–xxi*
Cloister Hotel 🏨, 7, 58
College of Charleston, 66, 70
Colonial Park Cemetery, 14, 15
Columbia, South Carolina, 4–5
Columbia Square, 14, 16
Computers, *xiii*
Concerts, 92
Confederate Museum, 72
Congregation Beth Elohim, 66, 70
Consumer protection, *xvi*
Crab Trap ✕, 56–57
Crafts and gifts, 44, 99–100
Crystal Beer Parlor ✕, 32
Cumberland Island, 49, 51–52
Cumberland Island National Seashore, 51
Cypress Gardens, 6, 101

D

Dance, 92–93
Davenport, Isaiah, 11, 14, 17
Days Inn Historic District 🏨, 87
Days Inn/Days Suites 🏨, 38
DeSoto Hilton 🏨, 37
Dinner cruises, 93
Dock Street Theatre, 68, 71
Drayton Hall, 78
Dune Deli and Pizzeria ✕, 91
Dungeness, 51

E

Ebenezer Church, 25–26
Edgar's ✕, 91
Edmondston-Alston House, 68, 71
1837 Bed and Breakfast and Tea Room 🏨, 90
Eliza Thompson House 🏨, 34
Elizabeth on 37th ✕, 6, 29
Elliott House Inn 🏨, 90
Elliott's on the Square ✕, 80
Emanuel African Methodist Episcopal Church, 66, 71
Embassy Suites Historic Charleston 🏨, 73, 85, 87
Emergencies, *xvi*
Charleston, 104
Savannah, 45, 47
Emmet Park, 14, 16

F

Factors Walk, 12, 16
Ferries, 63
Festivals and seasonal events, 8, 93–94
Film (cinemas), 94
Fishing, *xvi,* 102
Foley House Inn 🏨, 34
Forsyth Park, 14, 16
Forsyth Park Apartments, 21, 24
Fort Frederica National Monument, 56
Fort Jackson, 26
Fort Moultrie, 75, 76
Fort Pulaski National Monument, 26
Fort Sumter National Monument, 75, 76–77
45 South ✕, 29
Fragrant Garden for the Blind, 16
Francis Marion Hotel 🏨, 87
Francis Marion National Forest, 101
French Protestant (Huguenot) Church, 68, 71

G

Gardens, 6, 16, 78, 101
Gastonian 🏨, 34, 36
Gaulart and Maliclet Cafe and Restaurant , 82
Georgia
airports in, xii
bed-and-breakfast inns, xii–xiii

NOTES

NOTES

NOTES

Fodor's Travel Publications

Available at bookstores everywhere, or call 1–800–533–6478, 24 hours a day.

Gold Guides

U.S.

Alaska

Arizona

Boston

California

Cape Cod, Martha's
Vineyard, Nantucket

The Carolinas &
Georgia

Chicago

Colorado

Florida

Hawai'i

Las Vegas,
Reno, Tahoe

Los Angeles

Maine, Vermont,
New Hampshire

Maui & Lāna'i

Miami & the Keys

New England

New Orleans

New York City

Pacific North Coast

Philadelphia &
the Pennsylvania
Dutch Country

The Rockies

San Diego

San Francisco

Santa Fe, Taos,
Albuquerque

Seattle & Vancouver

The South

U.S. & British
Virgin Islands

USA

Virginia & Maryland

Walt Disney World,
Universal Studios
and Orlando

Washington, D.C.

Foreign

Australia

Austria

The Bahamas

Belize & Guatemala

Bermuda

Canada

Cancún, Cozumel,
Yucatán Peninsula

Caribbean

China

Costa Rica

Cuba

The Czech Republic &
Slovakia

Eastern &
Central Europe

Europe

Florence, Tuscany
& Umbria

France

Germany

Great Britain

Greece

Hong Kong

India

Ireland

Israel

Italy

Japan

London

Madrid & Barcelona

Mexico

Montréal &
Québec City

Moscow, St.
Petersburg, Kiev

The Netherlands,
Belgium &
Luxembourg

New Zealand

Norway

Nova Scotia,
New Brunswick,
Prince Edward Island

Paris

Portugal

Provence &
the Riviera

Scandinavia

Scotland

Singapore

South Africa

South America

Southeast Asia

Spain

Sweden

Switzerland

Thailand

Toronto

Turkey

Vienna & the Danube
Valley

Special-Interest Guides

Adventures to Imagine

Alaska Ports of Call

Ballpark Vacations

Caribbean Ports
of Call

The Complete Guide
to America's
National Parks

Disney Like a Pro

Europe Ports of Call

Family Adventures

Fodor's Gay Guide
to the USA

Fodor's How to Pack

Great American
Learning Vacations

Great American
Sports & Adventure
Vacations

Great American
Vacations

Great American
Vacations for
Travelers with
Disabilities

Halliday's New
Orleans Food
Explorer

Healthy Escapes

Kodak Guide to
Shooting Great
Travel Pictures

National Parks and
Seashores of the East

National Parks of
the West

Nights to Imagine

Rock & Roll Traveler
Great Britain
and Ireland

Rock & Roll Traveler
USA

Sunday in
San Francisco

Walt Disney World
for Adults

Weekends in
New York

Wendy Perrin's
Secrets Every Smart
Traveler Should Know

Where Should We
Take the Kids?
California

Where Should We
Take the Kids?
Northeast

Worldwide Cruises
and Ports of Call